Epic Fails in European History

Exploring Historical Missteps, Blunders, and Valuable Lessons of Europe's Past

Welcome Aboard, Check Out This Limited-Time Free Bonus!

Ahoy, reader! Welcome to the Ahoy Publications family, and thanks for snagging a copy of this book! Since you've chosen to join us on this journey, we'd like to offer you something special.

Check out the link below for a FREE e-book filled with delightful facts about American History.

But that's not all - you'll also have access to our exclusive email list with even more free e-books and insider knowledge. Well, what are ye waiting for? Click the link below to join and set sail toward exciting adventures in American History.

Access your bonus here

https://ahoypublications.com/

Or, Scan the QR code!

Table of Contents

Introduction

As the 2020s keep chugging along, it's becoming increasingly clear to everyone that humanity is once again living through historically decisive times, not just in Europe but throughout the world. Just like in centuries past, Europe is playing its part as one of the epicenters of major developments.

In such consequential times that have the potential to alter the course of history, it's paramount to remember the past, reflect on its many stories and lessons, and apply what can be learned to the present. History's missteps have been plentiful throughout the millennia, and studying them might be humanity's best hope for avoiding the same mistakes in the future.

The epic failures of European history have come in all shapes and resulted in varying degrees of catastrophe, so they often seem considerably different from each other on the surface level. However, some common themes begin to emerge once the underlying causes are put under a stronger magnifying glass. Above all else, these common themes have to do with human follies, which are often the driving forces behind disasters.

Historical events that might appear to have nothing in common can often stem from the same sources that are all too human. Hubris, arrogance, poor leadership, underestimation, faulty strategic planning, or a lack of critical thinking can sink civilian ocean liners or devastate entire armadas operated by massive empires. These and other inherent human factors can also spread deadly plagues, exacerbate famines, sabotage peace efforts, lead to industrial calamities, and much more.

The historical anecdotes in this book are more than a compilation. They are a string of case studies and lessons in human fallibility in all its forms. Of course, it would be unfair to attribute every single misstep in history solely to human error since fate has indeed often played its hand. Still, the unpredictable nature of fate is a natural force that is an eternal constant and gives no quarter to anyone. Yet, some people have an easier time navigating the stormy seas of fate than others.

This happens when people are able to escape the clutches of human error and conceit by making the right decisions. Avoiding recurrent human missteps is how individuals, communities, and nations have averted disaster throughout history, at least for a while longer than those who crashed and burned before them.

On a long enough timeline, virtually all human endeavors will crumble, but that doesn't change the fact that so many of the epic failures in European and world history could have been avoided. That's why studying and truly understanding history is so important, which is what this book will do by not just cataloging the failures but also examining the exact mistakes that led to them – and how they could have been avoided.

Chapter 1: The Titanic's Hubris and the Cavalry Calamity

In shipbuilding and warfare, opportunities have always been plentiful for great minds to demonstrate inventiveness and creativity. On the other hand, these ancient disciplines have provided room for all sorts of mistakes that have resulted in many major human disasters.

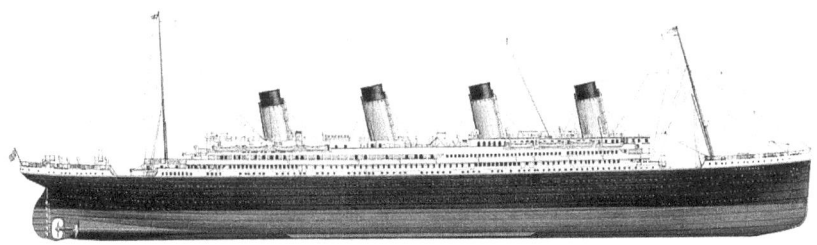

A diagram of the Titanic.

The sinking of the *Titanic* is a well-known example of how even the most impressive, groundbreaking feats of engineering are not impervious to fate. The *Titanic* is an excellent case study of how great engineering successes can sometimes inspire overconfidence, resulting in poor decision-making and planning, particularly due to a false sense of infallibility. Similar problems are common in warfare, but the chaotic whirlwinds of combat make it even more difficult to keep a clear head and make the right decisions. Sometimes, a simple communication error or misunderstanding can lead to disastrous outcomes, as in the case of the ill-fated British light cavalry charge during the Battle of Balaclava in 1854.

A Ship's Prestige and Downfall

The sinking of the RMS *Titanic* on April 14-15, 1912, is a story that requires no intricate introduction, but as with any ship, the *Titanic's* tale began at the drawing board and shipyard. It's not that anybody truly believed that this mighty ocean liner was unsinkable in the literal sense of the word, but the way the ship was constructed, her imposing size, and her design inspired tremendous confidence. For all intents and purposes, the largest ship on the seas at that time was seen as practically unsinkable.

Virtually Unsinkable

Unsurprisingly, most of the stories about the *Titanic* tend to focus on the eventual disaster and about 1,500 souls who perished with the ship. However, how the ship was envisioned and built also played an important part in her demise. More precisely, the impressive stature and enormity of the *Titanic* gave birth to her legend well before the disaster, and this prestige most likely played a part in some of the tragic decisions that made the sinking worse.

The impressive stature and enormity of the Titanic gave birth to her legend.
AnonymousUnknown author, CC0, via Wikimedia Commons.
https://commons.wikimedia.org/wiki/File:Titanic_Starboard_lifeboats.jpg

The dream of the *Titanic* was born in an era where cross-Atlantic travel was becoming more than just a matter of ferrying people between points A and B across the Great Pond. In the early 20th century, various shipping companies had already made their fortunes by transporting passengers and goods across the ocean, and maritime travel had become a perfected human trade because of it. Competition between these essential businesses was no longer as much about mere technicalities like speed and safety as it was about comfort. Building fast and powerful ships was still a key aspect of shipbuilding, of course, but passengers around 1907 were increasingly looking to not just traverse the ocean but enjoy themselves while at it. This was especially true for the wealthy clients, who had come to expect their journeys to entail all manner of luxury they were accustomed to.

To outdo competitors like Cunard Line and its impressive new liners such as the *Mauretania* and *Lusitania,* the British shipping company White Star Line needed something special in its fleet. Joseph Bruce Ismay had already turned White Star Line into a powerful company by 1907, but intense competition from his rivals pressed him to aim higher. In the summer of that year, Ismay decided to turn to the shipbuilders at Harland and Wolff out of Belfast, presenting his ideas to the company's chairman, William James Pirrie.

Ismay's requirements were simple. He wanted ships that were bigger and better in every way – and he wanted a fleet of them. It wasn't enough to just compete with White Star's rivals. In comparison, Ismay's ships had to make those of his competitors look small and obsolete. As they deliberated over dinner and drinks at Pirrie's London home, Pirrie began sketching according to Ismay's vision. An agreement was made to design and build three of the same ships: *Olympic, Gigantic,* and *Titanic.*

It wasn't long until the work began in Belfast, and Harland and Wolff amassed thousands of laborers for the monumental project. About Upward 15,000 workers were available on any given day at Harland and Wolff's impressive shipyard, and the bulk of them were tasked with the simultaneous construction of the *Titanic* and the *Olympic.* From 1909 onward, a core of around 3,000 workers was assigned specifically to the *Titanic* under the supervision of Thomas Andrews. As it gradually came into existence, the massive steel hull was an imposing sight at the Belfast shipyard. The ship's three colossal propellers were 23 feet wide, towering over the shipyard workers in historic photographs that are still admired.

The *Titanic's* title as the largest ship in the world at the time was a somewhat incidental result of the construction process. Both the *Titanic* and her sibling, the *Olympic,* were intended to be 882 feet long, dwarfing the main competition by over 120 feet. However, an unplanned nine inches over the original design length singled out the Titanic as the illustrious title holder during construction. Its fifteen bulkheads made of steel were particularly impressive, which provided for the fairly well-known, expectedly watertight compartments in the ship's interior.

The compartments and other aspects of the massive ship's design filled its builders with pride and confidence that the ship would dominate the seas even after sustaining damage to its hull. Looking at things from a historical perspective, it's possible that at least part of the confidence came from the fact that the North Atlantic had not seen a significant civilian maritime disaster in four decades. Perhaps complacency would be too strong a word, but the 40 years of smooth sailing in the North Atlantic would have certainly produced a sense that technology had advanced to a point where the sinking of a modern ship was rarely imagined. The *Titanic's* Captain, Edward John Smith, harbored similar ideas about modern shipping by the time his new, massive ship was launched on May 31, 1911.

The Disaster and Its Causes and Effects

The origin of the idea that the *Titanic* was unsinkable is difficult to ascertain, but the *Shipbuilder* magazine likely played a part. Other publications also closely followed the construction and launching of the marvelous vessel, as did a crowd of around 100,000 people who saw the *Titanic* make her first move into the River Lagan. After inspecting the ship and interviewing the builders, the *Shipbuilder* remarked that the ship seemed "virtually unsinkable." This was likely the characterization that later evolved into the colloquial idea that White Star had launched an invulnerable ship.

The *Titanic's* builders believed that even if their ship was pierced in a powerful collision, she would likely remain afloat because two entire compartments in its interior could be flooded without endangering the rest. Representatives of Harland and Wolff said as much to the press around the time the *Titanic* had embarked upon her sea trials and was about to begin her maiden journey.

Since the 46,000-ton **RMS** *Titanic* was such an awe-inspiring feat of shipbuilding, the main question has always been how it was possible for it to meet such a disastrous end on the night of April 14, 1912. In fact, this should be a two-part question. The first part is how exactly it sank, and that question has been easy enough to answer. The second, more difficult point of controversy has always consisted of all those avoidable ways in which the disaster was likely much worse than it had to be.

The *Titanic* embarked upon her tragic voyage shortly after being certified by the British Board of Trade, initially sailing to Southampton to load goods and passengers for the first time. On April 10, 1912, the magnificent new vessel left Southampton and headed to New York, and the rest is history. Officially, the **RMS** *Titanic* sank on the night of April 14 after colliding with a massive iceberg in the vicinity of Newfoundland. Historians agree that the disaster was the product of various factors, not just the collision.

For one, the massive ship likely sailed too fast, at 22 knots, which has been blamed on Captain Smith. The high number of icebergs was a known feature of that particular area of the North Atlantic, but that didn't dissuade the captain and his crew. One of the more infuriating theories, which may or may not have been a mere rumor, is that Smith was competing with the *Olympic,* trying to beat its crossing time in the Atlantic. Another more recent theory is that the ship's crew was contending with a fire in one of their coal bunkers, which required them to increase the sailing speed to full throttle.

To add insult to injury, the *Titanic* had been in contact with another ship in the area, the *Californian,* whose crew issued a warning about icebergs in the *Titanic's* path. A seemingly arbitrary misstep in communication caused the *Titanic's* crew not to take the warning seriously. Because the *Californian* failed to use the correct radio protocol, their message was interpreted by the *Titanic's* ratio operators as non-urgent, which meant that it wasn't immediately brought to the ship's captain.

According to some accounts, an equally simplistic navigational error could have also contributed to the disaster. The granddaughter of a senior officer and *Titanic* survivor, Charles Lightoller, claimed in 2010 that crewmembers steering the ship panicked when it became apparent that the ship was heading for a massive iceberg. Allegedly, the panic and confusion caused them to make a wrong turn and steer right into the iceberg instead of away from it. The foggy conditions and record-breaking tides in the area probably exacerbated the confusion and brought in an unusual amount of ice. Some of the more recent researchers believe that nature's hand was instrumental in the collision.

Three additional human errors were also at the heart of the calamity. First, after the wreck was finally discovered in 1985, studies on the ship's materials found that the builders of the *Titanic* had likely sought to cut costs during the construction. Particularly troublesome were the millions of rivets that held the hull's many plates in place. Tim Foecke and Jennifer Hooper McCarty studied dozens of rivets recovered by expeditions, finding that they had been smelted with too much cheap material, making them prone to fracturing. Researchers believe this was the main reason why the *Titanic* broke in half as she sank, making the disaster much worse.

Another tragic and perhaps mind-boggling oversight was the lack of binoculars issued to the ship's lookouts. In an apparently minor yet dangerous twist of fate, the officer in charge of the keys to the ship's binoculars storage had the keys in his pocket when he was transferred off the *Titanic* just before she sailed out of Southampton. According to some of the surviving lookouts, the additional binoculars could have been instrumental in helping the crew spot the iceberg in time. The keys were sold as memorabilia in the 2000s for £90,000.

In the end, no story of the *Titanic's* tragic demise is complete without what is perhaps its most controversial aspect. The *Titanic* didn't have enough lifeboats for everyone onboard, sailing out with just 20, enough to ferry only half the approximately 2,240 passengers and crew. The 20 lifeboats were enough to satisfy the legal minimum at the time, but inspectors in Southampton still advised the *Titanic* to increase the number of lifeboats by 50%. The advice fell on deaf ears since the crew and the operating company believed the ship would never need them.

The *Titanic* was supposed to rely on its 16 compartments and watertight bulkheads to take on significant water, even if pierced. In such a scenario, the ship was expected to stay afloat and use its state-of-the-art Marconi wireless telegraph to reach nearby ships for assistance. According to laws and doctrines at the time, the lifeboats on the ship weren't expected to house all of the passengers. Instead, they would be used as transports to gradually ferry the passengers to an assisting vessel.

Nothing worked as intended that night. The compartments gave way to water, and the ship sank in two hours and 40 minutes. The telegraph signals went unanswered because the closest ship, SS *Californian,* had signed off for the night, and the operator had gone to bed. The lifeboats were filled up frantically, in complete panic, departing with empty space that could have accommodated 400 more people, leaving over 1,500 to die with the *Titanic.* The catastrophe produced a furious firestorm of controversy, not just because of the lack of precautions but also because of the fact that many of the evacuees on the lifeboats secured their spots thanks to their class and status.

Besides all the pain and sorrow, the disaster did result in meaningful reforms. The International Convention for the Safety of Life at Sea soon introduced new regulations, requiring all ships to be fitted with enough lifeboats to house every passenger. This requirement was eventually elevated to 125% of every ship's capacity, demonstrating that harsh lessons of the past were indeed learned.

The Charge of the Light Brigade

The Charge of the Light Brigade is the name given to a military blunder that transpired during the Crimean War (1853-1856).

https://commons.wikimedia.org/wiki/File:Charge_of_the_Light_Brigade.jpg

The Charge of the Light Brigade is the name given to a military blunder that transpired during the Crimean War (1853-1856), which initially pitted Russia against the Ottoman Empire, joined later by a coalition made up of the United Kingdom, France, and the Kingdom of Sardinia to a lesser extent. The charge was a catastrophic frontal assault carried out by British cavalry units against well-prepared Russian positions on October 25, 1854. This unintentional suicidal attack has left a significant mark on British military history and is studied to this day.

The charge is pondered primarily as a case study of the importance of stable and clear chains of command, effective communication on the battlefield, and the indispensability of quality military intelligence. The incident occurred within the context of the Battle of Balaclava, in which the British Light Brigade, under the command of Lord Cardigan (James Brudenell), played just one part. The wider Battle of Balaclava was also a one-day engagement on October 25, which unfolded after the British tried to prevent the Russians from removing valuable artillery pieces from Ottoman positions that the Russians had previously captured. Brudenell's Light Brigade fought that day alongside another cavalry force, the Heavy Brigade, under Major General James Yorke Scarlett, and other military units, including some French forces.

On the opposing side, Russian infantry and cavalry, with significant artillery support, were waiting in prepared and well-defended positions. Under the command of Pavel Petrovich Liprandi, the Russians fielded around 20 battalions of infantry and more than 50 guns for fire support. Geography also played in favor of the Russians, enabling their heavy artillery to maintain fire control over three sides of what was essentially a very narrow valley. The narrow and relatively short valley acted as a funnel through which the lightly armored British cavalry would have to charge. The assault would never end well, but the problem wasn't that the British commanders were unaware of that fact.

The devastating charge was never meant to happen in that manner. It began when the army commander, Lord FitzRoy Somerset Raglan, ordered the overall commander of British cavalry forces, Lt. General George Bingham, to rush into battle and prevent the enemy from capturing the British guns around Causeway Heights. On paper, the mission was more than appropriate for the Light Brigade since light cavalry units were ideal for chasing and cutting down infantry, especially as they tried to withdraw while dragging massive artillery guns with them.

A Suicidal Frontal Attack

Lord Raglan's idea was for the cavalry to charge in, along with infantry support, with the Heavy Brigade playing its usual role of shock troops and the Light Brigade making a fast dash toward the Russian infantry evacuating the guns. At some point, when Captain Louis Nolan delivered the written order to Lt. General Bingham, crucial information was jumbled up and lost in communication. The idea that infantry was supposed to follow and provide support was obscured.

Bingham then asked the captain which guns his cavalry was supposed to charge at. Nolan's verbal interpretation of the order indicated that Bingham should send his men toward the numerous Russian guns at the far end of the valley. Nobody was ever able to ask Nolan how the misinterpretation happened because he died about one minute into the charge. Acting on the faulty order, Bingham ordered Lord Cardigan to charge into the valley with his 670 light cavalrymen.

Carnage ensued as the cavalry rushed toward the northern valley instead of Causeway Heights. Around 110 of the cavalrymen were cut down, blown to pieces, shot, or subjected to all manner of physical devastation. Another 160 or more were listed as wounded in action. The cavalry displayed tremendous courage in combat, as the suicidal elements of their order must have been apparent to these seasoned fighters. Records show no notable objections or insubordination. Ultimately, the Light Brigade's casualties amounted to around 40% of its manpower and likely around 400 horses.

While the Light Brigade was being butchered, Bingham and the Heavy Brigade initially tried to provide support and managed to flank and neutralize one Russian battery in the process. However, it wasn't long until Bingham, himself wounded, determined that the Light Brigade was in a hopeless situation and decided to pull the rest of his men out, leaving Lord Cardigan and his brigade to their gruesome fate.

Needless to say, the responsibility for this blunder quickly became a point of hot debate. A particularly troubling part of the story was the reported personal animosity between Bingham and Cardigan. James Thomas Brudenell, the Earl of Cardigan, was Bingham's brother-in-law, and some witnesses described the men as not being on speaking terms. Nominally, Bingham's decision to pull the rest of the cavalry out seemed like a choice aiming at reducing casualties in a hopeless situation. Still, the question of personal vendettas muddied the waters in many people's eyes, especially among the troops.

The remaining men of the Light Brigade, who could still ride, eventually managed to break through Russian attempts to encircle them and made their way home. Ultimately, the consensus is that the commanders principally responsible for the blunder were Lord Raglan as the commander-in-chief of the British forces in Crimea, Lord Bingham as the overall cavalry commander, and Captain Nolan as the man who may or may not have been responsible for the misunderstood orders.

The men in charge are easy enough to blame since their roles in the chain of command are well-recorded for all to see. The underlying factors of human fallibility that contributed to this British calamity are another topic entirely, and their analyses still persist. Of course, the most ominous and pessimistic interpretation of the events would be that the personal grievances between high-ranking officers might have contributed to the butchery of hundreds of troops forced to follow their orders.

Chapter 2: Constantinople's Fall and the Spanish Armada

History has been witness to quite a few powerful empires that commanded fear, respect, and admiration during their time. When an empire is at its peak of economic and military power, it's always difficult for people to imagine that such an immense force could simply dissipate and leave the world stage. Nonetheless, it always happens sooner or later; in many cases, there's hardly anything simple about the process. The Byzantines, as they are called now, were the perfect example of all this.

The fall of Constantinople.
dmytrok, ATTRIBUTION-NODERIVS 2.0 GENERIC, CC BY-ND 2.0
<https://creativecommons.org/licenses/by-nd/2.0/>
https://www.flickr.com/photos/klimenko/1437104919

On the other hand, the prestige of empires often gives birth to certain legends, which often revolve around certain strengths of major states that come to symbolize their might over time. England and Spain, which were both maritime superpowers in their time, came to be known for their naval supremacy. Their rule over the waves became synonymous with their immense strength and influence, but history has also shown how easily such prestige can be shattered.

The Old Empire's Final Chapter

The old-new Byzantine Empire is often misconstrued as its own new country, and an unfortunate number of people don't really know where it came from. In reality, it didn't come from anywhere. It was already there as an episode in a chain of statehood that stretched all the way to ancient Rome. That's because the term "Byzantine Empire" is a creation of more recent historiography, with the more accurate name for this state being the Eastern Roman Empire.

The "Byzantines," as they are often called, saw themselves and were seen by others as Rome, or at least a continuation of it. It was the last remnant of the old empire after the western portion collapsed in 476. The Byzantine name is very useful in today's historiography, as it helps separate this important and undoubtedly special phase of the Roman Empire from the rest of its long-state tradition.

The Byzantine Empire originated in Constantine the Great's decision to relocate his Roman capital to the city of Byzantium in 330, which was soon renamed Constantinople. 17 years earlier, the Edict of Milan had ended Rome's prolonged persecution of Christians and fundamentally changed the empire's relationship with the young religion. This enabled the Christian faith to spread more easily, and already in 380, the Edict of Thessalonica made Christianity Rome's official state religion. The final event that solidified the foundations of what would become the Eastern Roman Empire happened in 395, when Rome was split into the eastern and western administrative regions.

A statue of Constantine the Great.

As per the Romans at that time, the empire was still a unified, single state, but with two seats of power. After Western Rome collapsed in 476, the eastern portion was the only remaining part. It was still a vast empire, and as far as the people living in it were concerned, it was simply Rome with less territory. However, this land was dominated by the Greek language instead of Latin, and it began to develop along a new path now that Christianity was the dominant religion. With a different language, a relatively new state religion, a new capital on the Bosporus, and having been severed from the influence of the Western seat of power, it wasn't long until the Eastern Roman Empire took on a life of its own. Despite the state's clear and uninterrupted Roman continuity, referring to it as the Byzantine Empire from today's historical perspective is entirely justified.

The Long Decline

The Byzantine Empire outlived its western sibling by nearly a millennium. The historiographical consensus holds that Byzantine history extends from the capital's relocation in 330 to the fall of Constantinople in 1453. The Eastern Roman Empire went through several stages of strength and weakness, territorially expanding and contracting on numerous occasions over the centuries.

The fall of Constantinople can certainly be considered an epic historical failure, but in this case, it was hardly a singular incident with an easily identifiable culprit and a clear-cut blunder. Rather, the fall of the last Roman capital was the virtually inevitable conclusion to a prolonged period of decline. By the middle of the 15th century, the days of the uncontested Byzantine dominance across the Balkans, other parts of Europe, the eastern Mediterranean, and Anatolia were long gone.

In the centuries leading up to the final fall, many western territories were lost to emerging states in the Balkans, such as Bulgaria and Serbia. In the east, the territories in Anatolia were subject to constant warfare with the Seljuk Turks between the 11th and 13th centuries. These wars were gradually worn down the Byzantines, which resulted in the permanent Turkic settlement of Anatolia. The Seljuk Empire would also fall apart by the end of the 12th century, but the people it governed wouldn't go anywhere.

The last remnants of the Seljuk Empire were destroyed by the invading Mongols in the 13th century. After a period of strife in the region, the Ottomans rose to prominence in Anatolia under Osman I and began absorbing the other Turks in 1299. This was the founding of the Ottoman Dynasty, which would construct an empire that lasted until 1922. The consolidation of this new state in Anatolia was an immediate threat to the remainder of the Byzantine Empire, already weakened by the constant fighting with the Turkic settlers to its east. The year 1299 thus also marks the beginning of the Byzantine-Ottoman wars.

By the middle of the 14th century, the Byzantine Empire had already lost virtually all its territories in Anatolia. They only held onto certain areas in the eastern Balkans, minor possessions in Greece, and a piece of Crimea in the Black Sea. Constantinople remained under Byzantine control, but the capital was now at the eastern edge of their territory, exposed to constant Ottoman pressure.

Many other misfortunes were befalling Constantinople at that time. The Black Death hit the city in the late 1340s and cut down half of its population. Already contending with constant territorial losses and relentless pressure on all sides by Bulgarians, Serbs, Latins, and Ottomans, the bubonic plague dealt a devastating blow to the Byzantines. All these factors made life in Constantinople less desirable and economically attractive, further accelerating population attrition.

Around the middle of the 15th century, the once mighty and revered empire had been reduced to the city of Constantinople on the Bosporus, a few square kilometers around it, and disconnected territorial possessions that seemed increasingly beyond reach. The Ottomans had already broken through deep into the Balkans by 1450. Constantinople and the Byzantine territories adjacent to it were now surrounded only by the Ottomans and the seas. With the Ottoman Empire poised to move in and finish off the last remnants of their long-term imperial rival, it was clear that the fall of Constantinople was only a matter of time.

Rather than a single blunder, the fall of the Byzantine Empire is better seen as a case study of the transience of empires. In its heyday, the Eastern Roman Empire wasn't just feared and respected but admired. For many, it was a beacon of education and enlightenment, the heart of the Eastern Orthodox Christian world, and something to aspire to. To see what it had shrunk down to by the mid-15th century would have certainly seemed unbelievable and apocalyptic to students of history at that time.

The Siege and Its Consequences

The siege to end it all finally came in 1453, concluding on May 29 with Sultan Mehmed II's triumphant entrance and eventual looting of the city. Constantinople was a formidable fortress throughout its history, and it had endured many attacks before the final Ottoman siege. The city's powerful fortifications, the Theodosian Walls, played their part for centuries, and the city was also in an advantageous position geographically. This was owed to the seas that protected the capital on two sides and the naval assets that patrolled the waters. This was why Constantinople held out for so long, even after the Ottomans had already penetrated the Balkans and conquered most of the Byzantine Empire's neighbors.

Constantinople had powerful fortifications known as the Theodosian Walls.
A.Savin, FAL, via Wikimedia Commons:
https://commons.wikimedia.org/wiki/File:Istanbul_asv2021-
11_img65_Walls_of_Constantinople.jpg

The army Sultan Mehmed II assembled for the siege in early April of 1453 numbered at least 60,000 to 80,000 men, according to current, more conservative estimates. Earlier estimates by historians placed that number as high as 200,000. Either of these estimates would have constituted a massive army at Constantinople's gates. The sheer size of the Ottoman army was impressive, but it was hardly anything that the ancient capital had not seen before. More disturbing to the defenders were the artillery capabilities the Ottomans had brought to bear.

The amount and the firepower of Ottoman cannons in this battle were groundbreaking in certain ways, especially the size of some of them. The largest of these artillery pieces could send a half-ton ball to a range of almost one mile. The bore's opening was one meter wide, and the sight of such firepower would have certainly had a psychological effect on the defenders. The Byzantines would not back down, however, and they simply gave no reply to Mehmed II's demand for surrender on April 5. The siege commenced the following day.

As the Ottoman Turks blasted holes in the walls with their cannons, the defenders put up six weeks of resistance, doing their best to plug the openings and fight back the infantry trying to make entry. Despite the stiff resistance, effective assistance from the Pope, and even some revolts in Anatolia, Mehmed II persisted in his attacks. However, after those first six weeks, Mehmed II offered the Byzantine emperor Constantine XI a chance to pay tributes in exchange for the Ottomans withdrawing from the siege. The Sultan most likely did this so that he could go back home and put down the revolts personally, but the offer was turned down, and this surely sealed Constantinople's awful fate.

During the final, all-out assault on May 29, the Byzantines even mobilized women and children in a desperate attempt to defend the city. In a disastrous blunder, one of the gates at the city walls was left open, which the elite Ottoman Janissaries immediately exploited. It cannot be known for certain whether this was treason from within or a fatal mistake, but it was surely the final nail in Constantinople's coffin.

For their resistance and spite, Mehmed II ensured that the population and garrison of Constantinople were severely punished. Constantine XI perished in the final battles as Ottoman troops stormed the city and, thus, died the last Roman Emperor, falling under the sword like a common soldier. Much about his death remains a mystery because he had purposely disguised himself as a regular soldier to avoid having his body defiled in any subsequent Ottoman triumph or parade. The emperor also had a chance to flee the city before it fell, but he chose to stay and die with his city.

Constantinople's ensuing sack and looting was the final act in the Ottoman-Byzantine wars – concluding 11 centuries of the Eastern Roman Empire. Many of Constantinople's inhabitants were killed during the sacking, while others committed suicide, but more than 50,000 were taken into slavery. This monumental historical event marked an era's end and another's beginning. It solidified the Ottoman Empire as the dominant power in the region and much of the world, with Constantinople as its capital.

This epochal shift is symbolized to this very day by the legendary church of Hagia Sophia, built in 537, which still stands in present-day Istanbul. The church was converted to a mosque shortly after the city was captured, with four massive minarets added centuries later. Nowadays, Hagia Sophia stands as a major world heritage site and is visited by many people who come to ponder the weight of history and the transience of imperial power.

The church of Hagia Sophia.

The Mighty Armada

In the 16th century, the Spanish Empire was a global superpower with enormous colonial possessions in the Americas and numerous territories throughout Europe, Africa, and the Philippines. The backbone of this mighty colonial power was its immense navy, which was one of the most formidable fleets in the world between the late 15th and early 18th centuries. At its height, the Spanish Empire was the wealthiest and largest empire in the world, but the competition in the imperial realm was tremendous.

The Spanish Armada's Origin

The Spanish Armada refers to a historical event and the Armada itself, a fleet that Spain's Philip II had assembled for a planned invasion of England in 1588. This ambitious military plan was born within the context of the prolonged and undeclared Anglo-Spanish War, which lasted between 1585 and 1604. It was a conflict that oscillated in intensity as the two imperial and colonial states faced off in a power struggle.

This ambitious military plan was born within the context of the prolonged and undeclared Anglo-Spanish War, which lasted between 1585 and 1604.

https://commons.wikimedia.org/wiki/File:Spanish_Armada_fireships.jpg

Spain's enormous colonial possessions had brought it tremendous wealth in the 16th century, but England remained a thorn in its side for several reasons. Beyond colonial competition, Philip II also took issue with England's departure from Catholicism. As the dominant Catholic superpower at the time, the Spanish had made it their mission to champion the Catholic faith worldwide, a well-known feature of their colonial expansion in the New World.

Furthermore, Philip II resented many aspects of Queen Elizabeth I's foreign policy, particularly her support for the Dutch Republic. These tensions escalated in 1585 after the Treaty of Nonsuch, which formalized English support for the Dutch rebelling against Spanish rule. As an additional and even more disruptive snub to the superpower, British and Dutch privateers engaged in piracy along numerous Spanish maritime trade routes. Sir Francis Drake particularly distinguished himself in these activities by attacking Spanish routes in the Caribbean between 1585 and 1586.

All these factors helped Philip II when the time had come to do something about the English and put an end to their interference. The wheels were thus set in motion for an invasion of England, with the main goals being the overthrow of Elizabeth I, the restoration of Catholicism, and ultimately Spanish political control over England. Had it been successful, the invasion would have likely resulted in the absorption of England into the Spanish Empire.

For the campaign, Philip assigned about 30,000 elite troops commanded by Alexander Farnese, Duke of Parma and Spanish regent in the Netherlands. These troops were stationed in Flanders and designated as the primary land forces for the invasion. The army would have to cross the Strait of Dover to invade England, which meant contending with the English fleet that patrolled the strait adjacent to the English Channel. This meant Spain would have to dispatch its naval assets to neutralize the threat and clear these waters.

Assembling this task force would take nearly two years, and the armada would come to around 130 ships. The fleet was to be commanded by Alonso de Guzmán, Duke of Medina-Sidonia. The Duke had no experience leading a navy or even a small fleet, but Philip II was confident in Spain's naval superiority. The confidence was certainly not baseless, as Spain had all but ruled the seas at that point, and its massive galleons were a force to be feared.

The Armada's Unseemly End

Confidence is one thing, but appointing an inexperienced commander to a major fleet and severely underestimating the enemy's capabilities implied something else. After its many successes in war, massive expansion, and acquisition of staggering wealth, it's possible that the Spanish Empire fell into complacency. Ultimately, however, the tactical flexibility and clever use of weapons would determine the outcome.

The Invincible Armada, as it was also known, set out from Lisbon in May of 1588. Its 130 or more ships carried 17,000 foot soldiers and about 7,000 crewmembers. Apart from having justifiable faith in the considerable naval and invasion forces, Philip II also had lofty expectations for what would happen in England. One of the hopes was that the army would be met by English Catholics and other sympathizers who would welcome the return of the church and assist in the overthrow of Elizabeth I.

The Duke of Medina-Sidona was ordered to enter the English Channel, crush any potential resistance from the English fleet along the way, and join up with the army in Flanders. After linking up, the armada would escort the Duke of Parma's army across the water and provide further assistance during the invasion. Opposing the Spanish was the English fleet in the port city of Plymouth. The English fleet was larger in total numbers, but the Spanish relied on their vessels being more formidable.

What they didn't account for, however, was how the English would use lightness and speed to their advantage. Not only could the English ships sail faster, but they were also easier to maneuver. The Spanish Armada came under attack as soon as it sailed into the English Channel, incurring casualties and inflicting none on the English. The inexperienced Spanish commander proved inflexible when he ignored sound advice from his officers to capture the Isle of Wight and consolidate a defensive position. In such a scenario, Spanish naval firepower might have been able to wear down the attackers, but Medina-Sidona chose instead to press on toward Flanders as ordered.

The armada's losses weren't significant, and they retained most of their strength by the time they reached Calais. There, Medina-Sidona chose to wait for a message from Parma and his forces in Flanders. The stoppage proved fatal as the armada came under a nighttime ambush, which forced the fleet to spread out, making them easy pickings. They took further casualties in the ensuing Battle of Gravelines, after which the remainder of the Spanish fleet managed to enter the North Sea and start making its way home around Scotland and Ireland. They were pursued the entire way, taking additional losses.

Poor planning, inflexibility, miscalculations, and weather conditions all played their parts in this defeat. The English proved themselves to be better tacticians in this engagement, using fire ships at night to cause chaos and making better use of their naval guns while maneuvering. The armada lost up to 20,000 men and, with only around 60 ships, made it back to Spain, but the Anglo-Spanish war continued for years afterward and was ultimately inconclusive. Being the most powerful state in Europe then, Spain's prestige also took a hit due to the disastrous attempt to invade England.

Chapter 3: The Maginot Illusions and London's Inferno

Epic blunders that change the course of history, whether in warfare or other human affairs, don't always result from people's inability to learn from history. Sometimes, genuine attempts to analyze past events, draw lessons, and make future preparations based on gained experiences can also fall flat.

One can know the history in intricate detail, but failing to understand how times change and lacking flexibility in strategic planning can be just as fatal as disregarding history altogether. France's formidable fortification system, known as the Maginot Line, is one of the prime examples of this. On the other hand, the Great Fire of London illustrates that poor planning and preparation can cause a minor incident to escalate into a calamity the likes of which nobody would ever expect.

The Maginot Line's Strategic Failure

The Maginot Line is one of the more famous tales of military history.
Made by Niels Bosboom, ATTRIBUTION-SHAREALIKE 3.0 UNPORTED, CC BY-SA 3.0
<https://creativecommons.org/licenses/by-sa/3.0>
https://en.wikipedia.org/wiki/File:Maginot_Line_ln-en.PNG

The Maginot Line is one of the more famous tales of military history. This is partly because it happened relatively recently, but it's also due to it playing a part in World War II. This epoch-defining war's influence in shaping today's world has made its many lessons particularly important and etched into humanity's memory. The Maginot Line remains one of the most thoroughly studied episodes in military history, particularly concerning defensive operations.

An Attempt to Learn from History

Contrary to popular belief, Maginot's intricate system of fortifications wasn't intended as an unbreakable barrier that would make France impervious to war. The common belief is that the French built these defenses with the expectation that a German army would attack exclusively through them, trying to cross the border directly. The reality is a bit more complicated than that, and the strategic planning behind the Maginot Line was undoubtedly more sophisticated and reasonable.

The Maginot Line was named after André Maginot, who served as France's Minister of War on multiple occasions between 1929 and 1932.

Another key figure in the Maginot Line's design was Paul Painlevé, who also served as Minister of War in 1925 and for a short term during World War I. He also held a number of other important posts, including Prime Minister in 1925.

These and other military minds sought to ensure that France could defend its sovereign territory more effectively in case another great war with Germany erupted. Scarred by the horrors of the Great War, France's primary goal was to ensure that the next war would not result in a stagnating frontline on its own territory. Although the German advance into France during World War I was stopped around 43 miles from Paris early in the war, the fighting became gruesome back-and-forth for much of the war's duration. The bulk of the Western Front's fighting took place along a wide frontline in northeastern and eastern France, wreaking havoc on much more than the armies involved.

Having lost 1.4 million soldiers during World War I, France was deeply scared by the conflict, as was much of Europe. On top of that, France had considerable previous experience with invasions from the direction of Germany, so the Maginot Line can also be seen as the final result of centuries of military incursions. Along this stretch of territory, France could hardly rely on any natural barriers to complicate enemy offensive operations, so a decision was made to do something about this problem.

Around the time when the Maginot Line was being conceived by strategists, there were two prevailing theories on the best way for France to defend itself in a future war, which was widely considered inevitable in the interwar period. The first proposal for the new defenses was advocated by the likes of Marshal Joseph Joffre, a distinguished veteran and overall commander on the Western Front until late 1916. His idea was to erect major fortified positions in those areas deemed to be of utmost strategic interest. This approach combined hardened points of defense with maneuver warfare, all inside France.

The second approach was advocated by Marshal Henri-Philippe Pétain, the victor at the massive 1916 Battle of Verdun. He preferred a long line of smaller fortified positions to protect a wide front and bog the enemy down in trench warfare. The final design of the Maginot Line combined these two main proposals, creating a long line of fortifications that combined massive fortress areas interconnected by smaller defensive positions.

Construction work on the Maginot Line began in 1929 and would go on throughout the 1930s, being concluded just a year before World War II officially began in Europe. This impressive system of defenses stretched for around 280 miles and was much more than a string of trenches and firing positions. The Maginot Line was a major undertaking of engineering, detailed planning, and technology. Indeed, nothing about the construction itself was outdated or obsolete. It was a sophisticated project that cost France billions of dollars, adjusted for inflation.

The line featured major fortresses, systems of underground bunkers, dense minefields, gun emplacements, and much else. The builders and planners accounted for massive and sustained artillery fire and chemical weapons, among other threats expected from the Germans. Extensive concrete work and around 55 million tons of steel were used to entrench the fortifications to near indestructibility. When the Maginot Line was completed in 1938, it inspired awe and was quite likely the most sophisticated fortification system in the world.

André Maginot was himself a veteran of the Great War, and he pushed the ideas of Joffre and Pétain among French government officials.

André Maginot was himself a veteran of the Great War, and he pushed the ideas of Joffre and Pétain among French government officials. This was despite objections by other strategists who favored a more modern approach. Among them were Paul Reynaud and Charles de Gaulle; de Gaulle was a legend of French resistance in World War II and the country's distinguished Cold War leader. These men felt that France's resources would be better spent investing in aircraft and armored vehicles to create a modern force capable of maneuver and combined-arms warfare. The Germans, who embarked upon a massive militarization campaign under the Nazi leadership in the 1930s, had already adopted that exact doctrine.

Old Strategies vs. New Tactics

Given the work, competent planning, and execution that went into the Maginot Line, the fortifications themselves were technologically sound, impressive, and formidable in every way. Regarding the line's obsolescence, the point of debate wasn't the construction project's execution but the strategic mentality behind it. More precisely, what French military planners expected the Maginot Line to do was, perhaps, a thing of the past. Despite the naysayers, those who inspected the line and were impressed included Winston Churchill.

By the time Germany attacked France in 1940, the German Wehrmacht had adopted new tactics and completely embraced maneuver warfare. Highly mechanized infantry units were to be transported to the frontline, following closely behind an armored fist consisting of massive tank formations, all under the cover of air support. The German Blitzkrieg is a broad topic and has been analyzed for decades, but one of its goals was to make deep thrusts into enemy territory and bypass precisely the kind of defenses that France had built with the Maginot Line.

French military planners did account for this to some extent, particularly when it became clear that the fortifications wouldn't be extended along the French border with Belgium. Having declared its neutrality in 1936, Belgium didn't agree with the idea of a fortified border with France. Based on their harsh experiences of World War I, the Belgians believed the fortifications would leave the small country isolated and abandoned to fend for itself. As a result, the French were well aware that the Germans were highly likely to go on a flanking maneuver and push into France through Belgium.

The impenetrable Maginot Line thus narrowed down the possible directions of a German attack, forcing the invading army into a funnel through Belgium. This would give France time to fully mobilize its armies and send them to meet the Germans before they could penetrate into French territory. Furthermore, unlike the French-German border, the route through Belgium provided natural barriers, notably the enormous Ardennes forest. Rough terrain, dense woodlands, and poor and sparse road infrastructure were all expected to slow down the Germans and buy France time.

Unfortunately, for French military planners, nothing went according to plan. The commander of the Wehrmacht's tank forces, Lt. General Heinz Guderian, was a World War II veteran who fought precisely in the Ardennes. He was well-acquainted with the terrain and was able to plot the most optimal attack route, which proved vital in the 1940 invasion. The German blitzkrieg moved faster than expected, and their maneuver warfare tactics proved vastly superior to those of the Allies.

The forces that the French dispatched to the north to stop the Wehrmacht were soon outmaneuvered and encircled, along with the British and other allied troops. This led to the famous events in Dunkirk, where the encircled allies were able to evacuate across the English Channel just in time to avoid complete destruction. As the Germans made their way deeper into French territory, they were able to attack the Maginot Line from behind, capturing around 500,000 prisoners of war.

France fell in six weeks, even though the Maginot Line was an awe-inspiring display of fortification works, impervious to air power and saturated artillery bombardment. It even featured amenities and various comforts for its garrison of troops. It provided a false sense of security to France as a whole and the troops manning their posts along the line. Ultimately, the extensive fortified system proved inflexible and helpless in the face of a dynamic enemy. So catastrophic was the failure of the French strategy that the Maginot Line remains a popular symbol of false security to this day.

London's 1666 Inferno

The Great Fire of London in 1666 was a particularly notable episode, and it offers a stark reminder of just how many things can go wrong in a short timeframe.

Long before the terrible destruction that London endured during the Blitz in World War II, the city had already experienced similar tribulations. The Great Fire of London in 1666 was a particularly notable episode, and it offers a stark reminder of just how many things can go wrong in a short timeframe. The fire also demonstrated how poor management, slow response, and panic can make things go from bad to cataclysmic within a single day.

Murphy's Law at Work

The Great Fire of 1666 wasn't just a catastrophe that suddenly emerged and shattered some carefree existence of 17th-century Londoners. It was a particularly sad twist of fate that inflicted an additional blow to a city that had already been struggling. Indeed, London went through a major outbreak of the bubonic plague between 1665 and 1666, the last significant outbreak of the long-recurrent blight that had started in Europe centuries earlier. During this short epidemic, London lost around 25% of its population, some 100,000 victims of yet another offspring of the 14th-century Black Death. Even though it paled compared to the nightmare days of the Black Death in 1346-1353, the outbreak was still devastating enough to be remembered as the Great Plague of London.

Historians largely agree that the plague subsided before the fire in early September of 1666. Very few Londoners must have expected that just as their city began to recover from the Great Plague, a Great Fire would erupt and cruelly kick the city while it was still down. Historical analysis shows, however, that a major fire was likely only a matter of time in 17th-century London. The conditions were set, with many things just asking to go wrong, and all that was left was for Murphy's Law to kick in.

For one, London's city planning was very old, and the city's heart was built around a core that originated in the Middle Ages. The city's obsolete plan wasn't suited for housing the capital's swelling population, and this was a problem even after the plague wreaked havoc. The city's authorities tried to address some fire hazards, such as prohibiting the use of wood and thatch to build buildings and lay down roofing. The new rules were hardly enforced, though, as the population grew rapidly and those cheap materials were more widely available than brick and stone. The latter, more fire-proof materials were found mostly at the very center of the city, used to build the larger, luxurious homes of the wealthy elites and merchants. Everything around this small city center was overcrowded, built out of wood, and densely stacked.

King Charles II tried multiple times to get the local government to prevent the fire hazards from worsening, if not eliminate existing ones. In a practice that was a well-known fire hazard at the time, houses along narrow streets and alleys featured protruding second floors that sometimes extended far enough to almost touch each other above the streets. In 1665, the king tried to get local officials in the city to arrest people who had continued these practices when building new structures, but to no avail.

These and other problems in London's planning made it easy for a fire to start and spread, but some factors made firefighting efforts and evacuations more difficult. The old Roman wall, for instance, surrounded the medieval City of London, leaving eight narrow gates as the only paths of escape. The number-one problem for potential firefighting was the narrowness of the streets. On top of this, the streets and alleyways were crowded with carts, wagons, stands, and thousands of people. The panic that would erupt with a major fire would make this problem infinitely worse.

Fires in the city had become quite common by 1666, but recurrent incidents always ended with successful suppression. The firefighting methods of the time relied on a system of around 1,000 men on nightly fire watch shifts, which would alert a local church if a fire erupted in any home or building. The church would then use bells to assemble a group of local volunteers to suppress the fire. Water, strategic demolitions, and a variety of tools were the staples of London's firefighting system, and the system usually worked.

The purpose of demolitions was to create firebreaks by leveling the burning building or, if need be, buildings in the fire's path. This was usually done with tools like so-called firehooks, other hand-held tools, and even gunpowder. Equipment was usually stored at churches and readily available. In general, London's extensive experience with fires produced an intricate and fairly sophisticated firefighting system, but the procedures would prove insufficient when faced with poor leadership.

The Fire of the Century

The catastrophe started as a minor incident on September 2 when a bakery in Pudding Lane caught fire during the night. The fire began to spread rather quickly, and a party of firefighters from the local parish assembled within the hour. As the building was swallowed by the flames, the first responders determined that their best course would be to begin planned demolitions around the burning building. The locals protested, and the final word to begin had to be given by Lord Mayor Sir Thomas Bloodworth.

By the time Bloodworth arrived on the scene, the surrounding buildings were already ablaze, with the fire threatening to spread toward the warehouses, full of untold amounts of flammable materials. Whether out of panic, complacency, or plain incompetence, Bloodworth's historic reaction was a simple remark: "A woman could piss it out." This was a direct-enough answer to the experienced firefighters at the scene, who implored the mayor to begin demolitions.

The dry conditions after weeks without rain made the cramped wooden structures easy pickings for the fire, now exacerbated by strong winds. Hundreds of houses were consumed and began collapsing in no time, and the firefighters were still limited to using buckets of water to fight the emerging inferno. Accompanying the escalating fire was an outbreak of panic, prompting thousands to rush toward the river in an attempt to evacuate by boat. To make matters worse, spectators from the countryside around London began arriving to observe the unfolding chaos.

Demolitions to starve out the fire only began when King Charles II was informed of what was going on. Unfortunately, the order came too late, and the groups of firefighters with the usual tools could not demolish structures fast enough. Half the city was alight within two days, with thousands mobilized for the firefighting effort, including the king himself. As the firefighters began using gunpowder to hasten the demolitions, panic-fueled rumors began to spread that the French were invading.

Although it quickly became clear that no invasion was taking place, locals began seeing suspicious foreigners engaging in sabotage at every corner. It didn't matter that this wasn't happening, as the seed of fear had long been planted. Paranoia erupted within the context of the ongoing Second Anglo-Dutch War, and it wasn't long until mobs of infuriated Londoners began attacking French and Dutch immigrants. After four days of turning the city into ruins, the Great Fire was brought under control and mostly extinguished on September 6.

The Great Fire of London was the most destructive fire incident in London's history. The vicious firestorm laid waste to the medieval City of London and blazed through the capital with a trail of desolation in its wake. The human cost of the fire has been the object of some discussion and speculation. Historians such as Stephen Porter and Adrian Tinniswood argued that the blaze directly killed less than 10 people. The descriptions of the fire and its sheer scale, as Samuel Pepys and John Evelyn chronicled, have made such beliefs somewhat controversial. Historian Neil Hanson, for instance, disagreed with the low casualty estimates and felt that deaths caused indirectly by the fire should also be counted.

Whatever the true number of the souls who perished might be, the consequences of the Great Fire were enormous and far-reaching. St. Paul's Cathedral was completely destroyed, along with 89 churches and a significant part of London's housing, leaving hundreds of thousands homeless. Some good things came out of the disaster, though, as the city was given a chance to rebuild in a more organized, fireproof manner under the guidance of Sir Christopher Wren. London was reborn in the decades following the fire, laying the foundations for the city it is today.

Chapter 4: The Third Defenestration of Prague and the Misled Child Crusaders

When it comes to understanding the human phenomenon of war, the two most frequent areas of focus are its causes and its horrors. The strange thing about the way wars are triggered is that it's hardly ever the work of a single factor. Indeed, wars usually result from a sequence of events that can stretch across decades or even centuries, but there's often a clearly identifiable, singular event that serves as the initial spark that sets the wheels of destruction in motion. Among Europe's many horrific wars, the Thirty Years' War stands out as a particularly horrendous episode. Amid all the religious intolerance and fervor that led to this catastrophic European war, the 1618 Defenestration of Prague is often identified as the trigger.

In terms of the horrors that war inflicts on humanity, one of this great evil's most striking manifestations has to be the use of children. While this topic is unfortunately still depressingly relevant in the modern world, it's hardly a recent phenomenon. A particularly interesting case study of this symptom of warfare in Europe was the so-called Children's Crusade, which occurred in the 13th century. The looming factor of religion and its importance in European history is a thread that binds the following two stories together.

The Seeds of a European Catastrophe

Defenestration is a term that defines the act of throwing someone out of a window, and there's nothing figurative or ambiguous about it.

https://commons.wikimedia.org/wiki/File:V%C3%A1clavBRO%C5%BD%C3%8DK-Defenestrace.jpg

Defenestration is a term that defines the act of throwing someone out of a window, and there's nothing figurative or ambiguous about it. The term's first recorded use was in 1619, describing a scandalous event that transpired in Prague in 1618. That particular defenestration was a single violent episode in which two Catholic royal governors and their secretary were thrown out of one of Hradčany Castle's windows in Prague.

The Kingdom of Bohemia, which was the predecessor of today's Czech Republic, was at that time a part of the Holy Roman Empire. This disjointed and loosely confederated state accounted for much of Central and Western Europe. By the 17th century, these lands were embroiled in strife and tensions brought on by religious turbulence in the wake of the Protestant Reformation. Beginning in the 16th century, the Reformation shook the existing order in Europe to its foundations, especially in regard to the Catholic Church and its hold over the spiritual affairs of Central and Western Europe.

The Defenestration(s) of Prague

Although the 1618 incident in Bohemia was the first to be referred to as a defenestration, it wasn't the first such incident in Prague. In fact, there were three, occurring in 1419, 1483, and 1618. That's not to say that people being defenestrated was a rare occurrence at any point in European or world history. People being thrown out of windows, whether by raging mobs or on government orders, was and still is a relatively common human pastime.

What distinguishes the three Prague defenestrations is that they were all governmental and important enough to be entered into historical records. The 1483 defenestration was the least historically significant of the bunch, while the first and third are remembered as catalysts for prolonged religious conflicts in Bohemia and beyond. The 1419 incident led to the Hussite Wars, also known as the Bohemian Wars. The 1618 scandal produced so much outrage and international political backlash that it resulted in one of the most horrendous, religiously motivated rampages in European history.

In the lead-up to the third defenestration, Bohemia was going through a rebellious phase marked by various disputes with the ruling Habsburg Dynasty. The foundations of this prolonged friction were mostly religious. Just a year before the defenestration, Catholic officials in charge of Bohemia began cracking down on local Protestant construction projects. In a particularly controversial episode, Protestants in Broumov and Hrob were prevented from building chapels.

Closing down these construction sites was a violation of existing agreements that had kept the peace since 1609. The early days of Catholic Habsburg rule in Bohemia, which began in 1526, depended on a fine balance between the state's Catholicism and the widespread Protestantism of the local population. The Habsburgs sought to keep the peace by not forcing their subjects to convert. To that effect, the Holy Roman Emperor, Rudolf II, who also served as the King of Bohemia, gave the Protestants even more liberties in 1609. These rights were enshrined in the *Letter of Majesty,* which was Rudolf II's attempt to solidify his rule over Bohemia by giving concessions to the people in the face of growing competition from other Habsburgs, notably his brother, Matthias.

Matthias succeeded Rudolf II as the ruler of Bohemia in 1612, but he chose to continue his brother's policies toward the Protestants. Rudolf's decrees allowed Bohemian estates or local officials and nobles to openly practice their Protestantism. At that point, Bohemia practically had its own Protestant state church. Matthias continued to expand upon these religious liberties, but he was getting old and would not rule for much longer. Matthias was succeeded by his cousin, Ferdinand of Styria, in 1617. Ferdinand, a devout Catholic and fervent opponent of the Reformation, gradually started to bring the hammer down upon Protestantism in Bohemia.

The Third Defenestration and Its Consequences

Count Thurn.
Willem Jacobsz Delff, CC0, via Wikimedia Commons:

When Protestant estates of Bohemia protested the cessation of the construction of their chapels, Ferdinand abolished their assembly. A delegation of Catholic representatives arrived in Prague for a meeting on the morning of May 23, 1618. Led by Count Thurn, the members of the abolished assembly sought answers from the four Catholic regents. They were primarily concerned with whether or not the regents had personally participated in the anti-Protestant decisions of the emperor. The estates had previously compiled a letter they read during the meeting. In the letter, they emphasized that they had no intention of compliance and were prepared to stand up to the emperor's decisions even if it was to cost them their health and life. They referenced the imperial letter that was sent to the Catholic lord regents, asking if any of the present regents were aware of or contributed to it in any way.

The regents asked to be excused for the time being to go back and consult their superiors, after which they would respond via mail. Their request was rejected. The Protestant lords then allowed two regents, Matthew Leopold Popel Lobkowitz and Adam II von Sternberg, to leave. The Protestants presumed that these two men had no hand in the imperial order and excused them due to a level of mutual religious respect. Count Vilem Slavata of Chlumu and Jaroslav Bořita of Martinice, along with their secretary, Philip Fabricius, were told to stay. The two remaining counts were well-known for their staunch Catholicism.

The two regents then confessed to partaking in the letter and violating the Letter of Majesty's agreements – and unrepentantly so. The Catholic counts didn't hesitate to make their statement because they assumed they would merely be arrested and probably subsequently released. This, however, was a major misinterpretation of the prevailing mood among the Protestants.

Count Thurn then faced the Catholic regents and told them, as if proclaiming a sentence, that they were enemies of Bohemia's people and religion and a plague upon the crown's Protestant subjects. He then turned to a gathering Protestant crowd, proclaiming that the three imperial representatives had to be killed in the name of justice and to preserve the Protestant faith and its rights in Bohemia. The Protestants then threw all three men out of a third-floor window.

In a miraculously comical twist of fate, this act turned out to be a double blunder. All three of the victims survived falling 70 feet (21 meters) to the street below. In the ensuing firestorm of controversy across the HRE and beyond, Catholics interpreted this as divine intervention, arguing that the regents and their secretaries were saved either by angels or by the Virgin Mary herself. Protestants argued the point, suggesting instead that they were saved by falling onto a heap of manure.

Unfortunately, things would not end with a heated yet humorous clash of interpretations of the event. Instead, Protestants and Catholics began mobilizing for a major war. Ferdinand of Styria was crowned the Holy Roman Emperor as Ferdinand II in 1619, with the Thirty Years' War already having erupted by that time. The estates of Bohemia nullified his rule of Bohemia and appointed Calvinist Frederick V as his replacement. This was ultimately an illegal action, which meant Bohemian Protestants could not expect international support. In the first major war battle at White Mountain in 1620, the Protestants were defeated, and Ferdinand's Catholic rule over the Kingdom of Bohemia was restored.

The reprisals were brutal, including the sacking of Prague and gruesome public torture and execution of Bohemian nobles and citizens in the town. The heads of the slain were hung up on hooks to be displayed as an ominous warning. This was a single, early episode in a war that ravaged the continent until 1648. Through wanton destruction, countless battles, and devastating outbreaks of disease in the ravaged countryside, Europe would lose up to 8,000,000 people in the war. This would be an unfathomable cost even in proportion to today's much higher population numbers, but in the 17th century, the war was cataclysmic.

Children's Crusade

There is a somewhat common misconception that wars in the Middle Ages were primarily the endeavors of the nobility, with peasants and other lower classes serving as unwilling participants who never had a choice. Forced conscription has certainly been around for as long as organized warfare, but the history of medieval war is nowhere near that simple. In reality, many of the wars that were fought back then, just like in recent times, have enjoyed extensive popular support, with entire populations willingly participating and volunteering for battle.

When it comes to the deeply unsettling phenomenon of child soldiers, coercion is even more common and reprehensible. Nonetheless, history has still shown plenty of examples of children willingly joining the war effort, although it's much more difficult to talk about consent when it comes to young kids. The so-called Children's Crusade, which most likely transpired in 1212, is an example of how the fever of war and misguided dreams of glory can infect young minds and lead them on foolish adventures that end in tragedy.

A Product of the Zeitgeist

The story of the Children's Crusade is part history and part legend, mainly because a lot of the facts surrounding the event have been difficult to ascertain.

The story of the Children's Crusade is part history and part legend, mainly because a lot of the facts surrounding the event have been difficult to ascertain. This attempted campaign was a popular Crusade, which meant that the Catholic Church didn't officially sanction it. It was one of several such Crusades, organized by regular people, usually peasants, inspired by popular enthusiasm for crusading in the Holy Land. Without authorization from the Church, these Crusades were essentially organized mobs that sprung up multiple times between the

11th and 16th centuries. From a historical perspective, such attempts illustrate the popularity of crusading among the lower classes across Europe.

Two boys dreamed up the Children's Crusade of 1212, Stephen of Cloyes from France and Nicholas of Cologne from Germany. Nicholas of Cologne was certainly very young, but his exact age is unknown. Stephen of Cloyes was most likely only 12 years old. According to the traditional narrative, the boys inspired thousands of others to follow their lead, and some estimates have placed the number of recruits at around 20,000. Many were kids like Stephen and Nicholas, but the makeshift peasant army also included adolescents and adults.

The dream was very simple, albeit incredibly ambitious. The boys and their self-proclaimed army of crusaders expected to do a better job than professional crusaders, perhaps counting on their unmitigated fervor and devotion to Christendom. The ultimate goal was to capture Jerusalem and restore Christian rule over the Holy Land. Unfortunately, for the young would-be crusaders, the lack of an official papal sanction meant no resources and money would be allocated to support their campaign and its lofty goals.

This bizarre movement sprung up within the context of a series of Christian defeats, particularly in the Third and Fourth Crusades, which happened in the late 12th and early 13th centuries. Jerusalem fell to the Muslim forces of Saladin in 1187, and this recapture of the Holy Land by the forces of Islam sent shockwaves throughout the Christian world. The disaster inspired a widespread desire across Europe to drive the Muslim armies out of the Holy Land, which precipitated the Third Crusade.

The Third Crusade, beginning in 1189, was an organized military campaign that headed for the Holy Land but eventually got bogged down and defeated before ever reaching Jerusalem. The Fourth Crusade, which began in 1202, was an even worse embarrassment for the armies of Christendom. On their way to the Holy Land, the Crusaders took a detour toward the Balkans, sacking Constantinople and fighting with several other Christian powers in the region.

All these defeats would have undoubtedly demoralized many people across Europe, but for many, they only added fuel to the flames. Across Europe, the dream of restoring the cross over Jerusalem continued going strong, and it was especially powerful in young and impressionable minds, as is often the case with dreams of glory in war. Many Europeans felt frustrated with the failures of the Crusaders and began doubting the competence and even the motivation of European monarchies to carry out this holy task. However, it wasn't just a religious sentiment, as many of the European peasantry had invested taxes and resources, whether voluntarily or by law, into the Crusades. People wanted a return on their material and spiritual investments, so much so that some started thinking that they should take matters into their own hands.

An Adventure Never Meant to Be

That's probably how two boys in 1212 got the bright idea to avenge all of Christendom with their own sweat and blood. It all began in the spring of that year, a strange time in the French region of Vendôme. Children began spreading rumors that some local kids were receiving divine visions telling them to embark upon a great Crusade to avenge Jerusalem. Stephen emerged as the ringleader, although he was but a humble shepherd. The traditional legendary narrative holds that Stephen talked to France's King Philip II personally, telling him of a letter he had received from Jesus Christ. The supposed letter didn't specifically instruct the boy to go on a war of conquest, but it told him to preach the cause and build a following. Expectedly, the king shrugged off such wild claims, sending the boy home.

Simultaneously, a similar phenomenon occurred in Germany, with Nicholas from Cologne amassing his own following based on similar claims. Medieval sources are unclear as to whether or not these two boys were in contact or even knew of each other at that time, but given the sociopolitical and religious climate of the time, it's possible that both movements emerged spontaneously. As the vigilantes mobilized their sympathizers, it's also uncertain whether they set out on the journey together or if they linked up at some point after making their way across Germany and France.

The goal of the Crusaders was to march into Italy and arrive at Genoa, where the bulk of their "forces" could board ships and set sail toward the Levant. It's also possible that some smaller groups splintered off, trying to carve their own paths toward other ports in Italy and France. This long march quickly became grueling for all these unfortunate, imaginative children and any potential adults who might have gone with them. With no official support to provide logistics and supplies, the little Crusaders had to improvise and rely on donations or charity as they went along. As soon as the children tried crossing the Alps, disaster began to strike on all sides, causing many of them to starve to death or collapse from exhaustion. Many adventurers became disillusioned with the whole undertaking and departed the group.

Those who persisted did eventually make it to Genoa, but their dreams of a glorious Crusade were shattered when it turned out that they couldn't afford transportation to the Levant. The locals weren't particularly supportive or helpful either. Some of the medieval writings suggest that the child Crusaders might have expected that God would split the Mediterranean and clear a path as He did for Moses at the Red Sea, but no miracles transpired that day.

Various versions of the story differ as to what happened after that, with one story stating that the children were granted an audience with the Pope, who just told them to go home. A much darker narrative says that the rabble of attempted child Crusaders was soon broken up, with kids being shipped off to various lands and sold into slavery. Of course, there's no hard evidence to prove or disprove this account. Nowadays, it has been suggested that the tragic ending to the story was somewhat fabricated by the Church and purposely disseminated across Europe as a cautionary tale to other foolhardy youths who might get similar ideas. This unfortunate mob of youthful medieval thrill-seekers, with no equipment, weapons, or official sanction, dissolved under the waves of history, never coming close to the Holy Land.

Chapter 5: The Flawed Peace of Versailles and Vasa's Doomed Voyage

Humanity's most hopeful ideas and attempts can often crash and burn or lead to outcomes completely opposite of what was expected. This can be true in all human affairs, including politics, international relations, state-building, and engineering. Things can take unforeseen twists and turns and flip all expectations upside down due to mistakes that are difficult to identify until after disaster strikes.

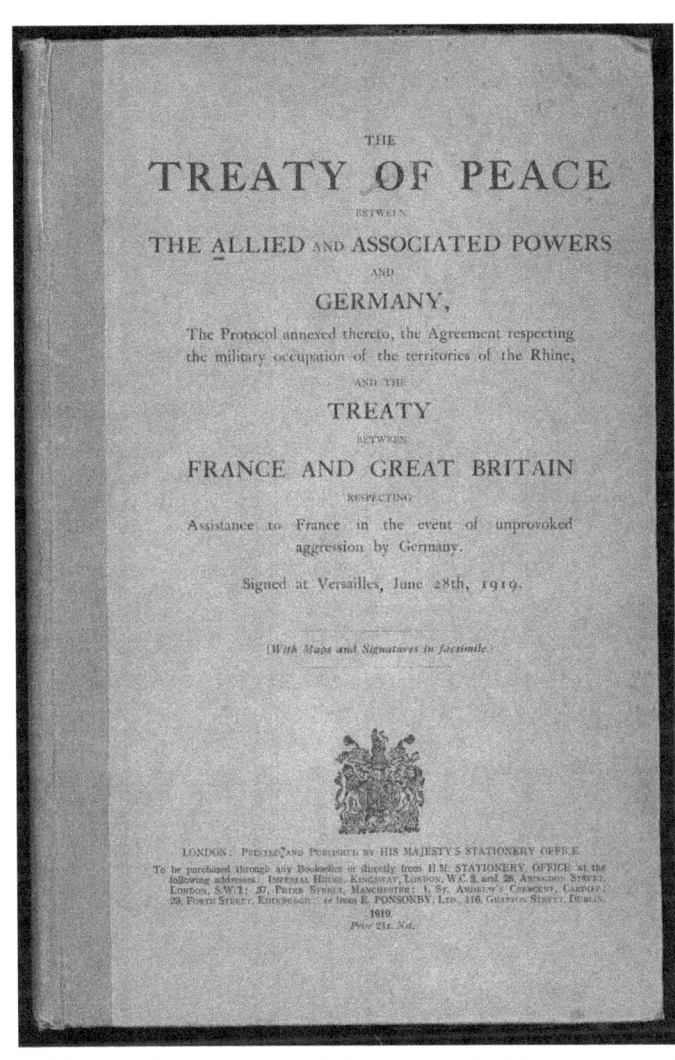

The Treaty of Versailles is nowadays regarded as a case study of how important it is to build peace on solid foundations.

The Treaty of Versailles is nowadays regarded as a case study of how important it is to build peace on solid foundations. Interpretations of its historical role differ, of course, but many see it as a geopolitical blunder of epic proportions. The irony of peace leading to war is a bizarre enough thought, but that's undoubtedly a fair way to analyze European affairs in the wake of World War I. It can be equally preposterous to suggest that a carefully designed ship hailed as the latest word in maritime engineering can sink within 20 minutes of being launched, but that is indeed what happened with *Vasa*. Humanity's accomplishments are many, but many stories remind the world that, as the old adage says, man plans while God laughs.

A Peace Treaty Done Wrong

After the guns finally went silent on November 11, 1918, Europe was a dreadful landscape of ruins and graveyards. Peace reigned over the battlefields, but the entire continent was collectively traumatized despite the relief. The enthusiastic militarism with which most of the European powers went to war in 1914 was completely gone, and the people's only concern in the wake of this apocalyptic conflict was how to never do it again.

At some point in the course of the Great War, the gravity and scale of Europe's butchery must have sunk in because many Europeans during that time famously referred to the conflict as "the war to end all wars." Even before the ceasefire, Europeans could hardly fathom the idea that a bloody disaster so gruesome could ever befall the continent again. It was simply unthinkable that such unprecedented destruction and human suffering could fail to teach a valuable lesson, yet that's exactly what would happen.

An Attempt at Europe's Deliverance from Warfare

World War I concluded with the widely celebrated Armistice of 11 November 1918, setting the stage for further negotiations and agreements regarding the post-war order in Europe. A long-awaited peace was somewhat secured with this armistice, but there was a lot of work to be done to ensure that Europe could build lasting peace. This prolonged process is referred to as the Paris Peace Conference, which began in early 1919 and lasted until the following year, with additional negotiations and meetings taking place all the way to July 1923.

Although the war was generally a grueling stalemate on the Western Front with occasional back-and-forth, Germany and the Central Powers ultimately lost. Much of the fighting happened along a frontline inside French territory, and it often seemed like Germany had the upper hand. However, with the general exhaustion and the 1917 entry of the United States into the war, the writing was on the wall by 1918. The most immediate and visible consequence of the ensuing peace processes was the dissolution of many major European powers. Russia had already plunged into revolution and internal warfare in 1917. Next on the chopping block were the Ottoman Empire, Austria-Hungary, and the German Empire.

Germany was hit particularly hard by the defeat. In 1914, Germany's territory in Europe stretched far to the east of its present borders, including a big chunk of present-day Poland and beyond. Germany also had many colonial possessions in Africa, East Asia, and New Guinea. These overseas territories were quickly divvied up among the Western Allies for their own colonial empires, but European Germany was also subject to territorial concessions.

It's noteworthy that German elites in 1914 were so eager for war against their European adversaries, especially France, because of Germany's comparatively unsuccessful colonial expansion. Throughout the 19th and early 20th centuries, Germans harbored a chronic resentment against the major Western colonial powers because they felt sidelined and reduced to minor expansion, whereas the British and the French commanded vast colonial dominions worldwide. At the onset of World War I, which was a time of widespread nationalism in Europe, German leaders and a great chunk of the population were in agreement.

The war was a way for Germany to take its "place under the sun," as Foreign Minister Bernhard von Bülow described. The conflict was precipitated by numerous and complex causes, not the least of which were the Sarajevo assassination and rampant imperialism and militarization by all major European powers. Still, Germany's own unfulfilled ambitions were a major factor in the German rationale behind the war. As a result, the seizure of German colonial assets, as per Article 119 of the Treaty of Versailles, was a slap in Germany's face, but that was just a sweetener.

Shattered Dreams of Peace

In the days leading up to the Armistice, a communist revolution erupted in Germany, or rather its first phase, which lasted between October 29 and November 9. The impending defeat in war, the countless casualties, and the deteriorating economic situation culminated with an uprising that effectively abolished the German Empire. Kaiser Wilhelm II abdicated shortly afterward, and Germany was reconstituted as the Weimar Republic by the summer of 1918.

This new democratic state had to contend with complete devastation in the country and try to rebuild Germany from scratch. However, the Treaty of Versailles stipulations made that difficult job even harder. One of the most controversial aspects of the treaty was the enormous reparations that Germany was forced to pay the Allies, particularly France. Germany was essentially labeled as the sole aggressor and instigator of the war, having to pay damages that came as a consequence. The reparations had to be paid in gold, ships, and various other forms, amounting to around $269 billion in today's value.

Apart from having to relinquish valuable European territories, Germany was also obligated to abolish conscription and maintain an army of no more than 100,000 men. They were also barred from procuring any armored vehicles, military aircraft, or submarines. The Weimar Republic was allowed to operate a maximum of six battleships in its navy. During the Paris Peace Conference, U.S. President Woodrow Wilson presented his famous Fourteen Points to ensure a long and just peace in Europe, but the European Allies wanted compensation. They also wanted to ensure a long peace not by reconciliation but by making sure that Germany would have no capacity to fight.

President Woodrow Wilson presented his famous 14 points.

The modern weapons of World War I, which included chemicals, made this conflict the most destructive war in history by that point. Proportionally speaking, the casualty rates weren't unheard of, but the firepower available to the warring parties and the speed at which masses of people died in excruciating trench warfare were unprecedented. The Armistice and the peace processes from 1918 onward did stop the war, but the fact that it was ultimately a botched peace undoubtedly constitutes one of the most depressing failures of European and human history.

These humiliating terms laid the seeds of resentment in Germany right from the start. The disgruntled population and political leaders detested the Allies and their conditions, but they also quickly began directing their scorn at those who agreed to such terms and the Weimar Republic as a whole. For many Germans, the humiliated and dysfunctional republic felt like little more than a containment chamber imposed by Germany's enemies.

On the global stage, the treaty also led to the Covenant of the League of Nations, the brainchild of Woodrow Wilson and other like-minded leaders. This was humanity's first failed attempt to create an international system of accountability and order, which would emerge again as the United Nations after World War II. Germany joined the League in 1926 and would remain a member until the rise of Adolf Hitler in 1933.

As the late 1920s rolled around, the Great Depression hit. This was the final straw for many Germans in the struggling and unstable Weimar Republic. Streets were awash with protests, activists of all creeds, and brawls between communists, monarchists, and, increasingly, a new movement under Adolf Hitler. In these tumultuous years in defeated Germany, many people certainly believed in a democratic future, but the Weimar Republic simply wasn't delivering results. Far more disgruntled were the millions of prideful Germans who wanted answers as to why their country had to bear sole responsibility for the carnage of the Great War.

The people wanted answers, justice, a better life, and the restoration of dignity that they felt was stripped away from their country. As time went on, more and more of them wanted vengeance. Hitler was one of many radicals during those days but was also an excellent orator with a clearly articulated vision for German greatness. Without a crystal ball to see the grim future that would follow, Germans resonated with the message. Hitler also knew how to crystalize and harness the people's anger by focusing it on a clearly defined culprit, for which he chose the Jews and various other elements.

Apart from a failed attempt to violently overthrow the Weimar Republic, the rise of Hitler and his Nazi Party mostly occurred within the confines of the democratic process early on. After the party finally rose to power in the 1930s. However, Hitler was quick to dissolve democratic institutions and the Weimar Republic itself. As the Third Reich ascended in the doomed republic's place, Germany soon left the League of Nations and began a massive rearmament program. Less than 20 years after the end of World War I, Europe was already gearing up for the next major confrontation.

The blunder of Versailles was in humanity's inability to stop the carnage in the long term, making the treaty a missed opportunity for all of mankind. In a twisted historical irony, the peace of the interwar period caused a new, even worse war. The Treaty of Versailles offers a valuable lesson in peace-building, illustrating that signatories must restrain their hatred and their own geopolitical ambitions. Peace is always preferable to war, but a peace process must be just to provide a foundation for lasting, healthy relations and prevent a future disaster. Even more important is never to take peace for granted and to find ways to preserve the progress and international institutions humanity has worked so hard to establish since 1945.

Vasa's Disastrous Debut

Of all the mighty feats of engineering, shipbuilding has, for a long time, been one of the most important human activities in terms of propelling civilization forward. When early humans began migrating out of Africa 60 to 90,000 years ago, they likely used land bridges that have long since sunk beneath the rising seas. As a result, nature had complete command over where humans could and couldn't expand. That has changed dramatically since people developed the ability to navigate across the water on primitive boats and early ships just a few thousand years ago.

Everything changed when the era of seaborne migrations began, allowing humanity to reach the level of interconnection and global communication that's taken for granted nowadays. Shipbuilding developed in leaps and bounds over the subsequent millennia, going from primitive boats to massive galleys relying on oars, sailing ships, steamships, and eventually nuclear-powered leviathans that rule the waves nowadays.

An Impressive Feat of 17th-Century Shipbuilding and Its Short-Lived Glory

Sweden's Vasa was not the largest ship but was meant to pack the biggest punch.
Dennis Jarvis from Halifax, Canada, CC BY-SA 2.0 <https://creativecommons.org/licenses/by-sa/2.0>, via Wikimedia Commons: https://commons.wikimedia.org/wiki/File:Sweden_1011_-_Vasa_(4033812152).jpg

Somewhere along that journey of progress, Sweden's *Vasa,* also called *Wasa,* was supposed to be her own minor shipbuilding revolution in 1628. The history of Swedish naval power stretches back more than 500 years as officially recorded, although the preceding Vikings were pioneers in this field centuries before that point. By the 17th century, Sweden was a major European power that ruled much of the area around the Baltic Sea.

At the peak of this power, King Gustav II Adolph commissioned a massive warship that would strike fear into Sweden's European competitors while also serving as a mighty symbol of strength. The job of building *Vasa* was bestowed upon Henrik Hybertsson, a distinguished Dutch ship designer who worked in Stockholm at that time. The ship was named after Gustav II's dynasty, and, as such, it had to be not just formidable but also a masterpiece.

At 226 feet (69 meters) in length, it wasn't the largest Swedish warship, but it was meant to pack the biggest punch. The ship was fitted with a total of 64 guns, which was an absolute record at that time, and it immediately established *Vasa* as one of the world champions of naval firepower. The vessel's body was thoroughly decorated with extensive ornamental carvings, sculptures, and reliefs, which told epic stories of the Vasa dynasty, its history, and the stories of Gustav II Adolph himself. As a result, *Vasa* was just as much a message as she was a naval asset.

Unfortunately, the things that made the ship so impressive to look at would eventually become her downfall. The 64 guns that the ship carried far exceeded the 36 she was designed for. The entire gun deck weighed heavily on the ship and caused major instability, threatening to turn the vessel over on its side. The extensive and lavish ornaments likely also contributed to the ship's unbearable encumbrance. The root of the problem is difficult to determine long after nearly four centuries, but it's possible that such an enormous engineering project was beyond the capabilities of the people assigned to it.

The design flaws were bad enough, but the king also wanted to present and ceremoniously launch his marvelous new ship as soon as possible, exerting undue pressure on the builders to hasten their work. The big reveal came on August 10, 1628, at the Stockholm Harbor. Crowds of onlookers, officials, and the king assembled to witness *Vasa's* launch on her maiden voyage. The ship was scheduled to ferry several people over to a fortress before proceeding to assume her duties as the flagship of the reserve squadron at Älvsnabben.

It was barely 20 minutes after the ship's departure that trouble began, still within visual range of the spectators. The unstable vessel struggled with strong winds and seemed to want to tip over to the side. *Vasa* endured the first gust, but a second, stronger blow turned her over. At that point, *Vasa* began quickly taking on water and promptly sank, taking some 30 passengers and crewmembers with her to the bottom of the Baltic.

This massive embarrassment prompted an immediate investigation. A 17-member special commission was appointed by the king and headed by Admiral Carl Carlsson Gyllenhielm, the king's older half-brother. Just as they were during the ship's construction, engineers, naval officers, and crewmembers were reluctant to speak. Shipmaster Göran Mattson eventually cracked and admitted that problems with *Vasa* had been identified a whole month before launch. Ordered by Captain Söfring Hansson and witnessed by Vice Admiral Fleming, a demonstration involving 30 crewmembers running across the deck showed the ship was woefully unstable. Nobody dared to spoil the king's ceremonial launch, however.

While the mighty *Vasa* turned out to be a spectacular naval failure and an embarrassment to Sweden and its Crown in the 17th century, the ship found a second life as a treasure trove of archeological discoveries. She was found and finally recovered in the 1960s, almost intact, along with over 40,000 invaluable artifacts that had sunk with the vessel. The few parts that had broken off from the ship were also brought up, and the vessel, which is really a work of art, was fully restored. Since 1990, *Vasa* has been displayed at the Vasa Museum in Stockholm and can still be enjoyed as the best-preserved warship from the 17th century.

Chapter 6: The Great Famine's Shadow and the Confusion at Karánsebes

Some of the worst disasters in human history have come in the form of famines. In the 21st century, people in the developed world think of famines as something that happens only in the world's poorest regions, if even there. However, in reality, famines used to be much more common throughout the world less than a century ago.

Just like horrible major wars or plagues, some of the most destructive famines have killed millions and altered the history of entire nations and regions. Some were caused by human mismanagement, while others were the result of natural causes. In some instances, both of these factors worked in unison to produce catastrophes of unbelievable proportions, as was the case with the Irish Potato Famine.

Still, when it comes to disasters resulting from mismanagement, war is perhaps the ultimate setting where such misfortunes can run rampant. The confusion and chaos of war provide conditions where a million things can go wrong due to the slightest misstep. Sometimes, the missteps are so extreme that the resulting calamities simply boggle the mind. One such episode that isn't very famous was the Battle of Karánsebes, a blunder so ridiculous that it would have been comical if it didn't result in so many deaths.

The Irish Potato Famine

The Irish Potato Famine, also known as the Great Famine or the Great Hunger, happened between 1845 and 1852. This period of Irish history had enormous ramifications and altered the nation's history in numerous ways. It was a terrible example of how a natural disaster can worsen when human incompetence, mismanagement, and even malice are allowed to state their case.

An Irish Catastrophe

By the 19th century, the people of Ireland had come to rely on potatoes as a diet staple. In retrospect, this lack of diversity in their food sources probably made the island's 8.5 million inhabitants vulnerable to disruptions in the food supply. Around half of the population was getting almost all of their nutrition exclusively from potatoes, which certainly wasn't a bad choice of food in terms of what it offered. For one, potatoes were easy to grow across Ireland despite its unpredictable weather patterns and rough terrain, making them cheap and accessible even to the poorest farmers.

Secondly, potatoes are a rich source of nutrients like carbohydrates and vitamin C, making them a solid dietary staple. However, the Irish overreliance on potatoes in the mid-19th century wasn't necessarily a choice. For millions of families, potatoes were the only crop they could afford, but their choice of diet was also narrowed down by British policies. Ireland at that time produced more than just potatoes, but the central government in England would usually reserve the more valuable produce for export, leaving very little for domestic consumption.

Living in what was essentially a colony of Great Britain, Irish farmers didn't have much of a say in which of their yields they could keep and which had to be shipped out. This was because most of them didn't own the land they were working on, as much of the prime real estate was owned by British landlords. Many of these landlords didn't even live in Ireland. As a result, the native population could do little more than rent land from absentee landlords and follow their instructions on what to produce, hoping that enough food would be left to feed their families by the end of the season.

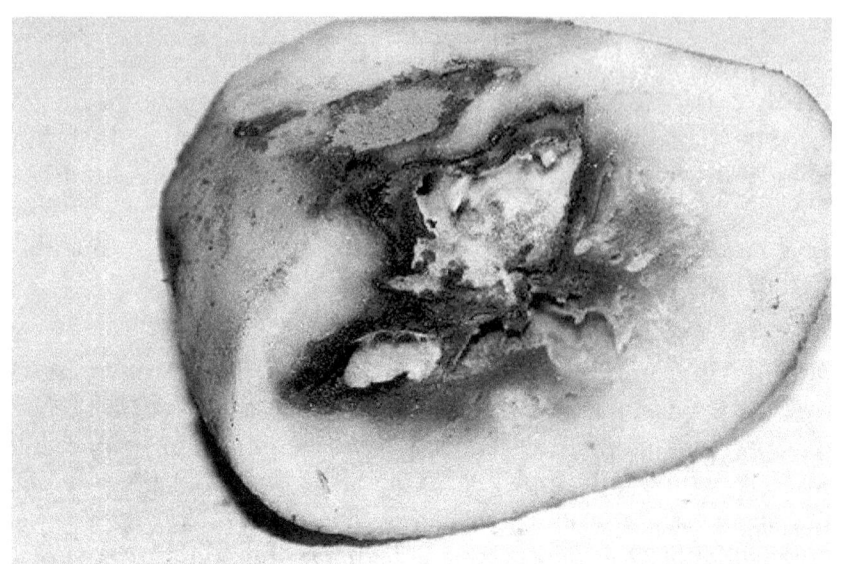

Phytophthora infestans is a type of fungus that causes potato blight to quickly spread all over the country.

I.Sáček, senior, CC0, via Wikimedia Commons:
https://commons.wikimedia.org/wiki/File:Phytophthora_infestans_5619.JPG

The first signs of trouble began with the arrival of "the blight" in 1845. Now understood to be caused by *Phytophthora infestans,* a type of fungus, this potato blight quickly spread and severely impacted potato crops all over the country. This potato blight was likely brought over by ships from America. The 1845 season in Ireland was particularly favorable to the fungus due to an unusually high humidity. The fungus quickly spread from crop to crop, and it wasn't long before it spread all over Europe, but the poor Irish countryside was hit particularly hard.

The biological causes behind the blight weren't understood at the time, but the effects were readily apparent to all. Potato plants gradually turned black above the surface, and the potatoes themselves often turned out shriveled up and black. Even those that looked normal on the outside were terribly rotten on the inside, filled with a slimy, decaying pulp whose pungent smell was enough to make one's stomach turn. The unlucky rural poor who still tried to eat these potatoes found themselves very sick, sometimes to the point of death. As the blight spread throughout the country, it became clear that Ireland's number-one dietary staple could no longer be counted on.

Escalation, Response, and Consequences

The failing crops initially struck the poor peasant class – who relied on potatoes for virtually all of their sustenance. Even though these people were reliant on potatoes, the emerging disaster could have likely been mitigated through appropriate measures. Other parts of Europe, such as Belgium and the Netherlands, weren't as reliant on potatoes, but it was still their management of the crisis that made sure the effects of the blight would be minimized.

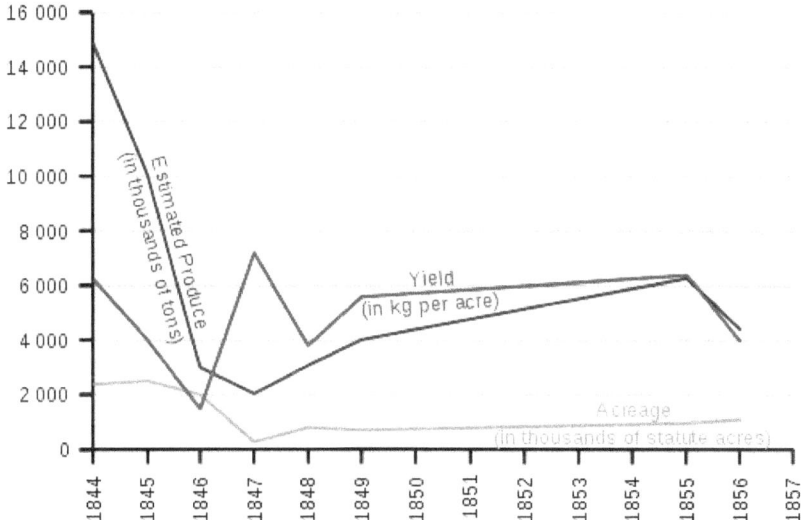

Potato production during the Great Famine. The failing crops initially struck the poor peasant class, who relied on potatoes for virtually all of their sustenance.

What began as a food supply crisis among the rural poor soon evolved into a national disaster, primarily due to Britain's inadequate response. Despite the growing number of people who were starving, the central government in London continued exporting Ireland's agricultural products. Instead of diverting some of this food to alleviate the ongoing famine, the British imported American corn as a substitute for the locals. The Irish peasants were also offered manual labor jobs on public projects, but none of these measures were enough.

Problems in the distribution system meant that a lot of the starving people in rural areas weren't getting their share, but even when they did, the corn wasn't enough. The vitamin C that the farmers were previously getting from potatoes was gone now, leading to an increase in instances of scurvy. Potatoes offered a wide range of crucial nutrients that made the population healthy, but now they were becoming vulnerable to all sorts of diseases other than scurvy, and Ireland's infant mortality rate increased sharply. All the while, the government kept exporting livestock and grain, which could have provided the starving populace with life-saving whole foods and meat.

The starving Irish people who were given British jobs on public projects were underperforming or outright collapsing due to the strenuous work, making it impossible for them to make money to buy food. Some workers had to walk 20 miles or more to their jobs, starved and exhausted before even beginning their labor. Workers would sometimes die on their way to work or home. This was a time of large families who depended on the agricultural and manual labor of the men in the household, who often fed up to ten children and their mothers. The death of just one father, if the children were young, would often doom his entire family.

In 1846, the second year of the famine, the blight got even worse, and even those families that somehow managed to survive unscathed were starting to feel the pain. As the famine worsened, the British government's response actually diminished. What little help came from international relief efforts was nowhere near enough. On top of that, the central government introduced new rules, making it more difficult for people to qualify for assistance. Worse yet, London increased taxes on Ireland to make them pay for much of the relief they desperately needed.

Despite the catastrophe, the government continued pursuing *laissez-faire* policies, greatly exacerbating the crisis. Historians nowadays blame these policies for the Great Famine, but the underlying reasons for such a callous British approach have been intensely debated. Religious intolerance and prejudice against the Irish among the British ruling classes are often cited as some of the key factors. Supporting these arguments are the many examples of how the British press and public discourse treated the famine.

The Irish were often portrayed as drunkards, sinners, and generally incompetent people who only had themselves to blame. The supposed laziness of the Irish was also a frequent prejudice that was widely propagated. These attitudes dehumanized the Irish, deflected responsibility from the central government, and made genuine relief efforts more difficult. Many government officials in London treated the famine as divine punishment that was being rightfully inflicted upon the Irish. More than just disparaging the starving Irish population, these bigoted beliefs motivated lawmakers to block numerous proposals that could have saved countless people.

During this time, the United Kingdom of Great Britain and Ireland, as the monarchy was known between 1801 and 1922, was immensely wealthy. The colonial superpower commanded enormous financial assets and resources of all sorts across its vast global empire. One million Irish people died between 1845 and 1852, not due to a scarcity of resources but of political will. The famine diminished only when natural conditions allowed for Ireland's potato crops to recover. The seven years of the Great Famine were a defining period in Irish history. Apart from the one million who died, up to two million more fled the country, mostly to America. All of these factors combined halved Ireland's population by the 1920s. For many Irish people, the suffering of those decades was the final straw, mobilizing public opinion in favor of independence. This culminated in the Irish War of Independence in 1919-1921 and the establishment of the Republic of Ireland.

An Entire Battle of Friendly Fire

The 1788 Battle of Karánsebes, if it should be called such, is difficult to classify. On the one hand, it was certainly a victory for the Ottomans during one of the numerous Austro-Ottoman wars. On the other hand, it's hard to pinpoint whether it was a victory or a defeat for the Austrians since two armies did fight, and one likely came out on top, but the problem is that both of them were Austrian. Indeed, this battle, often referred to as the "dumbest battle in history," was an episode of inadvertent infighting brought on by a friendly fire incident.

The Story as Told

The Habsburg-Ottoman War took place due to miscommunication.

The ill-fated engagement occurred within the context of the Austro-Turkish War, sometimes also called the Habsburg-Ottoman War, between 1788 and 1791. The Habsburg Empire, just like the Austrian and Austro-Hungarian empires that succeeded it, was a multi-ethnic monarchy with several Slavic and other minorities under its dominion. Likewise, the empire's armies were highly diverse, sometimes made up of disjointed units whose fighters could hardly understand each other. A unified command structure generally bridged that gap with success, but miscommunication might have played a part in the blunder at Karánsebes.

The battle took place when the Holy Roman Emperor, Joseph II, led an army of around 100,000 men into the territory of modern-day Romania to look for the Ottomans. In the vicinity of Karánsebes, the army established a campsite along the Timiş River just south of the town. What happened afterward has been the subject of some debate due to the scarcity of contemporary records. This might have been due to Austrian efforts to suppress information and bury the incident to save face.

According to the traditional narrative, after the army encamped itself on the western bank of the Timiş, they sent a scouting party made up of hussars across the river to collect information. While they didn't find any Ottoman troops, they did run into a number of local residents who were offering to sell schnapps. The hussars, worn out from their long march, were in the market. After purchasing the alcohol, however, they didn't hurry back to share it with their comrades, instead staying across the river and having a party.

When a group of Austrian infantry went after the hussars across the river, they found them in a festive mood, sharing drinks and entertaining themselves with the locals. The infantry troops wanted to join in on the fun, but their request for alcohol was denied by the hussars, who, by that point, were significantly intoxicated. The entire barrels of schnapps that the hussars had were jealously guarded, and the cavalrymen had allegedly set up rudimentary fortifications around the precious liquid. An argument erupted, quickly escalating into a brawl, at which point someone fired a shot.

The ensuing firefight was only an overture to the carnage yet to come. Hearing the sounds of battle, the bulk of the army soberly manning their posts around Karánsebes interpreted the ruckus as an Ottoman attack. This faulty information then made its way back to the drunken troops across the river, who interpreted it as a Turkish attack on Karánsebes, after which they rushed back to help their forces. Hussars and various infantry units began fleeing amid the chaos, with constant miscommunication along the way. Apart from German-speaking Austrians, the army included Romanians, Italians, Serbian frontiersmen, Croats, and a number of other groups.

As some of the hussar cavalry fled through the encampment, Austrian artillery units commanded by General Colloredo thought this to be a Turkish cavalry charge, ordering his guns to fire. As the rest of the drunken troops from across the river arrived to help, the approaching infantry was likely interpreted as an additional Ottoman attack, at which point the encamped troops opened fire. As the inebriated troops came under fire, they concluded that the camp and the town of Karánsebes must have been overrun and captured by the Turks.

As the carnage unfolded, some of the German officers likely realized what was going on, as the traditional narrative holds that they tried to stop the chaos by yelling, "Halt!" To the troops who didn't speak a word of German, this command to stop sounded more like Muslims calling out to "Allah" in the heat of battle, which only escalated the slaughter. By the time the fighting subsided, Joseph II was reportedly so demoralized that he ordered a complete withdrawal, providing a major opportunity for the Ottomans in the wider struggle to control the Danube.

Aftermath and Uncertainties

Ascertaining the number of casualties has traditionally been difficult, as with many other finer battle details. Traditional wisdom, which likely exaggerated the story, held that some 10,000 soldiers perished, but modern estimates place the number closer to 1,000. Such losses would still have been significant for a friendly-fire incident, seeing as the Austrians had nothing to show for their casualties.

When the actual Ottoman army arrived at the scene a couple of days later, they found a field strewn with the corpses of Austrian troops. The Ottomans had been preparing for a major battle to capture Karánsebes for a while by that point, but the sight of devastated enemy units made it clear that the conquest would be easier than anticipated. The Turks soon marched into Karánsebes and fortified themselves in the town, marking one of the easiest victories in all of Ottoman history.

The main issue with this account is that it's sourced from records that were compiled several decades after the event. It has been particularly difficult for historians to determine the length of the engagement and the number of casualties. The indications are strong that a significant friendly-fire incident and subsequent rout of the Austrian army had occurred primarily because it's known that the Ottomans captured Karánsebes without a fight. The Ottomans' easy and bloodless capture of such a strategic city would not have happened if the Austrians hadn't suffered considerable damage. It's also true that it would have been in the interest of the Habsburgs to keep the story out of public circulation for as long as possible.

One of the central questions has always been about how an organized army could engage in friendly fire for so long. The aforementioned language barriers among the troops undoubtedly played a major role. If it's true that the hussars stumbled upon a major supply of schnapps across the river, leading to the intoxication of hundreds of men, then these two factors could have easily made the situation uniquely chaotic.

This military campaign by Joseph II against the Ottomans was marred by various other setbacks. Outbreaks of diseases such as malaria and dysentery were particularly deadly, leading to the majority of the tens of thousands of casualties that the Austrians incurred. The Habsburgs eventually won the war and acquired new territories, so embarrassing tales such as that of Karánsebes could more easily be swept under the rug. Had the Austrians suffered a major defeat in the overall war, historians would have probably been more inclined to sift through all the setbacks, helping the disaster at Karánsebes make it into mainstream history sooner than it did.

Chapter 7: Napoleon's Blunder in Russia and the Spread of the Black Death

Of all the monumental events Europe has seen over the past millennium, few disasters and personalities stick out as much as Napoleon Bonaparte and the Black Death. While it's probably unfair to equate Napoleon with an outbreak of the bubonic plague, it's reasonable to say that both of these historic episodes have shaken Europe to the core and turned millions of lives upside down.

Napoleon had his motivations and ambitions and was ultimately just a man.

Napoleon had his motivations and ambitions and was ultimately just a man. As such, he could be understood and contended with, no matter how mighty he was. The Black Death, on the other hand, was a horrific force of nature that poses many questions to this day, let alone in the 14th century. As influential and powerful as one man can be, no human endeavor can match the turbulence nature can create if she chooses. Respectively, the stories of Napoleon and the Black Death are case studies of what it looks like when human beings and nature decide to flip an entire continent on its head, each in their own way.

The 1812 Invasion of Russia

A conventional interpretation of history among those who don't scratch much deeper than the surface holds that humanity has experienced two world wars. This simplified interpretation overlooks that there were a number of other wars that nearly satisfy the definition of a global conflict. In European history, the Seven Years' War, fought between 1756 and 1763, was perhaps the closest, with many historians considering it a world war.

On the other hand, the period of European history known as the Napoleonic Wars (1803-1815) is another example of a war that almost took on a global dimension. However, the conflicts consisted of seven individual wars, so they are rarely considered a single confrontation. Across those seven wars, dozens of countries faced off in numerous theaters and under varying coalitions, making this destructive period one of the most decisive in European history, with far-reaching global consequences.

Napoleon's Fateful Decision

One of the most infamous episodes in the Napoleonic Wars was undoubtedly the ill-fated invasion of Russia that the legendary military leader undertook in 1812. The invasion is also sometimes referred to as the Second Polish War, and it's known in Russia as the Patriotic War of 1812. At the helm of a 615,000-man invasion force known as the Grande Armée, Napoleon initiated an invasion of the Russian Empire that would lead to around 1,000,000 deaths in total. The invasion was a catastrophic defeat for Napoleon, who was considered all but invincible on the battlefield at that time.

In the years leading up to this military disaster, France and Russia weren't particularly hostile to each other. They did engage in warfare, but since the Treaties of Tilsit in 1807, the French and Russian empires were in an alliance. Napoleon secured this alliance in order to put pressure on his archenemy, the United Kingdom. The alliance that Napoleon had imposed on Russia obligated the Russians to participate in Napoleon's embargo against the UK, known as the *Continental System.*

Russia took on other obligations as part of the treaties, but it did get some benefits in return. France would support the Russians against the Ottomans and would step aside as Russia invaded Finland, which was then part of Sweden. On the surface, Tsar Alexander I of Russia and Napoleon had made an agreeable rapprochement, but the terms of the alliance were still favorable to France. The uneasy alliance was never going to last.

Due to past conflicts and grievances, in addition to further slights in the years after the alliance was formed, tensions escalated by 1810. The alliance fell apart late that year when the Russian Tsar officially left Napoleon's embargo due to its damage to Russia's economy. Napoleon was enraged and interpreted this move as a major betrayal. Within a year, he began making his preparations for war, through which he hoped to force the Russians back into the treaties.

The crushing defeat that Napoleon's Grande Armée would suffer in Russia is probably why many people harbor the false notion that the army marched into Russia unprepared. Napoleon was one of the greatest military minds in history and had a wealth of knowledge available to him. He studied previous invasions of Russia and was well-informed about the kind of land he'd be invading. Napoleon and his subordinates were also acquainted with the infamous harshness of the Russian winter.

In previous campaigns, the Grande Armée usually fed itself "off the land" by procuring provisions from the local populace. This wasn't possible in Russia because of how sparsely populated and vast the country is. Not only that, but the army would also have to contend with poor roads that were few and far between. Finalizing his preparations in the early summer of 1812, Napoleon expected the campaign to be wrapped up by the end of summer.

The End of Napoleon's Invincibility

One of the more visible mistakes in Napoleon's planning was that he, perhaps uncharacteristically, assigned important command positions to inexperienced relatives instead of proven generals. The Grande Armée was divided into three main fronts, the largest of which was deployed along the Niemen, a natural barrier and border with Russia then. On the other side, the Russian Empire commanded an army of some 650,000 men, although many of them were deployed elsewhere across Russia's immense lands. Only about 165,000 guarded the empire's western borders, facing off against close to 450,000 of Napoleon's troops.

Napoleon and his army, less than half of which was made up of Frenchmen, began crossing the Niemen on June 23, 1812. With this fateful decision, Napoleon didn't embark upon a war of conquest, planning instead to simply destroy Russia's military potential and force Tsar Alexander I into submission. This objective began to elude Napoleon from the moment his enormous army made first contact with the Russian Cossacks. These men on horseback exchanged a few sporadic shots with the French and quickly withdrew deeper into their territory as if to invite the invading army in. Bizarrely enough, the most notable event of Napoleon's entrance into Russia was his horse getting spooked by a rabbit and throwing him off, causing minor injuries to the emperor.

The essence of Napoleon's strategy was to move fast, outmaneuver the enemy, and take on individual Russian armies one by one, making them easy pickings. At his intended pace, Napoleon figured the campaign would be over in about three weeks, with a crushing defeat of Russia and with terror struck right into the bones of other European countries. The supreme commander of the Russian military, Mikhail Barclay de Tolly, saw through Napoleon's intentions.

The supreme commander of the Russian military, Mikhail Barclay de Tolly, saw through Napoleon's intentions.

The mighty French army soon found itself marching through endless plains, searching for a fight that continued to elude them. Napoleon seemingly had no alternative strategy, so he continued pushing into Russia, looking for an enemy who simply refused to fight. Napoleon knew that this enormous, sparsely populated land would make it difficult to feed his army on the move, so he brought massive amounts of supplies to sustain the campaign.

However, as the Russians continued to lure the invaders, the supplies began to run their course. The few settlements the Grande Armée encountered were found razed to the ground. Everywhere the French went, they found deserted, burned villages, and destroyed crops, livestock, and anything else that might be of value to an army. Despite protests from Russian officers who wanted to stand and fight, Barclay persisted in his strategy of attrition. As the French army waltzed into Minsk and Lithuania, the war that Napoleon wanted to wage continued to escape him.

The first notable engagement occurred a month into the invasion when Marshal Louis-Nicolas Davout defeated the Russians at Saltanovka. This defeat forced the Russians to continue withdrawing, but Napoleon's preferred timetable had slipped, and his army had incurred significant losses. Some were killed in combat, while others succumbed to illness brought on by a combination of heat and rain, costing the Grande Armée 80,000 men after only a single tangible military victory. Even before the first battle, desertion became a problem for Napoleon – and it would only escalate.

As the invading army pressed on, the only corpses they left in their wake were their own. The Russians had problems, too, particularly with infighting between Russian and Baltic German officers advocating different strategies. For many of the ethnic Russians in the army, Barclay's strategy of destroying and then handing over territory appeared increasingly traitorous. Barclay was eventually forced to begin offensive actions, and a period of direct engagements began in August of 1812.

Things came to a head during the Battle of Smolensk between August 16 and 18. The French did manage to beat back the Russians and capture the city, but the casualty ratio was almost 1:1, which meant further attrition for Napoleon's forces without much to show for it. At this point, Napoleon considered shifting gears and digging in for a prolonged war, making Smolensk a base of operations where he and his army would spend the winter. He decided against this idea due to the reputational loss it would bring by making it clear that the initial invasion had failed.

After the Russians withdrew from Smolensk and headed toward Moscow, the defeat caused a scandal in the Russian imperial capital of St. Petersburg. Barclay was relieved of his command and replaced by Mikhail Kutuzov, a man of great standing and experience on the battlefield against Napoleon himself. The new commander-in-chief continued the war of attrition until he finally gave Napoleon the massive battle he had hoped for. The Battle of Borodino took place on September 7, a turning point in the war.

Of the 300,000 troops that fought, around 80,000 were either killed or wounded. The casualties favored the French, but nowhere near enough to be sustainable. Napoleon had gotten the major battle he sought but failed to inflict the decisive blow. Kutuzov withdrew and left the road to Moscow wide open for Napoleon, yet the supposed victory was an anti-climax. The Russians still commanded a nearly intact army, and when Napoleon marched into Moscow, he found it abandoned and ablaze. Along with the 250,000 inhabitants who were evacuated, the Russian army even took the city's fire equipment.

As his starved army began to break down in the ruined city with little valuable loot, Napoleon waited for 36 days to be offered terms by Alexander I, hoping to salvage at least some compromise. No response ever came. Keeping an army stationed in the ruins of Moscow during the winter was unsustainable, so the French emperor decided to order a full retreat while autumn was still warm. The 100,000 men who remained in the Grande Armée could hardly imagine that hell had only begun.

Napoleon initially tried to retreat through southern Russia in the hopes of feeding his army, but Kutuzov prevented this, forcing the French to leave the same way they came. The retreating army was subject to constant ambushes and attacks by mobile Cossack units as they made their way through previous battlefields. The fields were littered by the Grande Armée's own unattended corpses, now decomposing and torn apart by wild animals. Winter came early that year, and temperatures had already dropped to -30°C in November. The ragged remnants of the once-formidable army marched on as they froze to death and fought among themselves over what little water and food they had left, even turning to cannibalism on a few occasions.

By the time Napoleon made it back across the Niemen in early December, his forces had taken around half a million casualties, 350,000 of them dead of various causes. The Russians also incurred significant losses, but the end result was hard to argue with. After crossing the river, Napoleon left Joachim Murat in charge and left for Paris to handle political matters, thus abandoning his battered army. A total of one million people died during the half-year campaign, making it one of the deadliest blunders in military history.

In the end, Napoleon's fatal flaw was underestimating the resolve of Tsar Alexander I and his people and how far the Russians were willing to go to achieve victory. On top of that, the enemy wasn't satisfied with just having banished Napoleon from their lands. Indeed, Russia went on its own offensive into Europe shortly afterward, linking up with Britain, Austria, Prussia, and other allies. A major push known as the War of the Sixth Coalition ensued, ending Napoleon's empire and sending him into exile, at least for a short while. Being the force of nature that he was, Napoleon returned in 1815, sparking the War of the Seventh Coalition, which finally put an end to his imperial ambitions at the legendary Battle of Waterloo on June 18, 1815.

Europe's Near Miss with Extinction

Well before the 20th century, Europe had also witnessed mass casualty events unrelated to war. One such catastrophe was the most infamous bubonic plague outbreak in history, known as the Black Death. This aptly named pestilence might have killed as much as half of Europe's population between 1346 and 1353. On a continent whose history is filled with virtually endless warfare, the Black Death was nature's way of reminding everyone that no powerful man, military leader, or armada can shake up the continent the way she can.

Such a devastating pandemic did more than just kill people. It triggered panic on an apocalyptic scale, making Europe tremble at its political, spiritual, and existential foundations. This historic natural disaster wasn't the blunder of any one person. However, it did highlight mankind's vulnerability to unexpected outbreaks of disease and how easily a horrific pandemic can spread among ill-prepared populations. Pandemics usually originate in nature, but they are made much worse through an endless series of daily personal blunders by people who don't know any better.

The bubonic plague was a horrifying disease. The written descriptions from the time of the plague and its aftermath spoke of a disease that mowed down everyone with ease, including young people in their prime. It usually started with awful fevers, vomiting, headaches, and painful joints. Without treatment, the disease had an 80% mortality rate, killing the afflicted within eight days. 14th-century writings tended to focus on macabre descriptions of that which could be seen.

Patients would develop buboes in their groin, neck, and armpit areas. The buboes or sores were festering boils that leaked pus and blood upon opening. They resembled tumors, some of which could grow to the size of an apple. These boils had a tendency to spread across the body as the disease progressed. Another common symptom of late-stage bubonic plague is the emergence of gangrene, rotting away tissue and skin and turning it black. People's fingers, hands, arms, and other parts would simply turn black and rot away, as on a corpse. The same blackness appeared on the buboes.

The bubonic plague comes from *Yersinia pestis,* a bacterium carried by fleas, particularly those that live on rodents. The Black Death pandemic likely included the pneumonic and septicemic plagues as well, which have even higher mortality rates, but the bubonic one was the most prevalent. By the time the Black Death arrived in 1346, Europe was already having a terrible century filled with war, famine, and outbreaks of disease.

The origin of the Black Death has been debated, but the most established theory holds that it formed somewhere in central Asia and China. The Mongols brought it from there into Crimea through warfare and trade, and then European ships picked it up and brought it to Italy. Ships have always been host to rats, which were perfect carriers for infected fleas. It only took around two years for the disease to flower out of Italy through trade, infecting much of Europe.

The existence of microorganisms like bacteria was completely unknown to humanity at that time, so treating the disease boiled down to herbs and other outdated methods. Prevention was also made difficult by non-existent sanitation standards and panic. When pestilence struck, God's wrath was a common interpretation. People would flee affected areas, helping spread the disease further and faster.

Within a couple of short years, many cities and towns across Europe were host to apocalyptic scenes with piles of corpses due to overcrowded graveyards. Those who chose to stay in place would shut themselves off, stay inside, and pray to God. Unrest, social breakdown, and mistrust ran rampant. Many people blamed the Jews and other outsiders, spreading rumors that they weren't getting sick, leading to untold atrocities. The pandemic sent reverberations throughout Europe's feudal system because so many farmers perished. It took around 200 years for the population of Europe to return to its previous number. The disease would recur numerous times during that time, albeit with less intensity.

It's tempting to assume that the superstition of the deeply religious medieval European society got in the way of reason and scientific understanding during the outbreak. Still, European civilization in the 14th century was undoubtedly sophisticated enough for its time, but humanity as a whole was simply more primitive and far from the scientific and medical breakthroughs that are taken for granted nowadays.

Even recently, humanity has been struck by several deadly and highly disruptive outbreaks. The Spanish Flu went on a rampage worldwide in the aftermath of World War I. In fact, the death toll estimates for the Great Influenza are the same as those of the Black Death. The flu was much less devastating in proportion to the world population at the time, but it clearly demonstrated that humanity still had to contend with dangerous outbreaks despite all the advancements in medicine and sanitation.

Even in the 2020s, the world was given a stark reminder of vulnerability during the COVID-19 pandemic. The recent and still ongoing pandemic has killed millions of people, wreaked havoc on the global economy, and created major social upsets all over the world. While COVID-19 is incomparable to the horrors of the Black Death, it spread incredibly fast and with troubling ease. Picturing what would have happened with a disease that was just as viral but much deadlier than COVID doesn't take much imagination. This recent reminder and the horrific lessons of history will hopefully help humanity better prepare for future outbreaks.

Chapter 8: Lusitania's Last Voyage and the Tunguska Mystery

Some historic events have left their mark because they irreversibly altered the course of major events. They are remembered as key points in a long chain of events that lead into today, which is why they have such weight. These turning points of history tend to be well understood, thoroughly studied, and forever debated, leaving very little to the imagination – but a great deal to interpretation. The sinking of RMS Lusitania is one such event.

On the other hand, some things have happened with so much mystery surrounding them that the mystery itself is enough to etch them into historical records. When an event isn't understood and leaves nothing but questions in its wake, it piques human interest in ways that most other historical information can't. People have a natural urge to seek answers, and when answers are elusive, legends emerge. One of these legends is the so-called Tunguska incident.

The Cruel Fate of RMS Lusitania

A little over three years after the sinking of the *Titanic,* Europe witnessed a new horrific maritime catastrophe when another British ocean liner, RMS *Lusitania,* was sunk on May 7, 1915. The ship was sophisticated for its time and held the title of the world's largest ship for a couple of months after she was launched in 1906. Operated by the Cunard Line, RMS *Lusitania* was also the record holder for the fastest time across the Atlantic in 1908. She had completed more than 200 cross-Atlantic trips by the time she was torpedoed by a German U-boat in World War I.

Europe witnessed a new horrific maritime catastrophe when another British ocean liner, RMS Lusitania, was sunk on May 7, 1915.

An Outrageous International Incident

The entirety of the *Lusitania* incident has always been controversial. One of the most immediate questions has always been whether or not the voyage should have happened in the first place. The ship would eventually be sunk off the southern coast of Ireland, which was – at that time – part of the United Kingdom in its entirety. To make matters worse, the *Lusitania* was officially registered as a British vessel.

The UK had been at war with the German Empire for quite a while by the time the *Lusitania* departed New York on May 1, 1915, returning to Liverpool. As such, the waters around Ireland and the British Isles were an active war zone involving a hostile country that operated a fleet of U-boats specifically designed to hide under the surface and sink ships. The Lusitania's voyage was universally known to be highly dangerous, leading to significant controversy before the ship even set sail.

Responding to concerns raised at the German Embassy in the U.S., the embassy published a clear warning to potential passengers. Germany stated unambiguously that nobody should board the *Lusitania* and that there was a high probability that a disaster would ensue. Germany, at this time, was under blockade by the British and French, which made all British ships fair game in their eyes. The warning was disseminated in the press on April 22, well before the ship's departure.

At this point in the war, the British Royal Navy was undoubtedly the dominant naval power, but the advent of new weapons and strategies began to level the playing field. The Germans pioneered submarine warfare during the Great War, wreaking havoc on enemy naval power as well as shipping lanes. The rules of engagement were fairly loose, particularly since the British would often employ civilian liners for military purposes if the need arose.

As RMS *Lusitania* closed in on the British Isles, things were going according to routine. Captain William Thomas Turner was confident that his state-of-the-art ship was all but invulnerable to submarine attacks due to her speed, and he assured the passengers that they had nothing to worry about. During the ship's approach, the British tried to provide RMS *Lusitania* with a naval escort. Unfortunately, problems in communication and issues with Cunard policies led to complications that eventually forced the ship to enter U-boat territory without an escort.

Disaster struck at 2:10 PM on May 7, just 11 nautical miles south of Ireland. One of the numerous German U-boats lurking beneath the British waves, SM *U-20,* commanded by Walther Schwieger, fired a single torpedo, getting a direct hit on RMS *Lusitania.* Just like the *Titanic,* the *Lusitania* was expected to take hours to sink in the event of any damage, giving passengers time to evacuate to a rescue vessel via lifeboats. To everyone's shock, the fatal hit by the German submarine sunk the ship in eight minutes.

The probable reason why the ship plunged to the depths so fast and suffered such damage from a single torpedo was a second explosion that rocked the vessel shortly after impact. The ship's hull was completely devastated, and it keeled over on one side at a very sharp angle in no time, causing complete pandemonium across the ship's six floors. Despite the crew's best efforts, there was nowhere near enough time to organize an effective evacuation. Only several of the ship's 48 lifeboats managed to load passengers and launch.

Controversies and Ramifications

One of the most immediate effects when the news of RMS *Lusitania's* demise broke was that the disaster opened people's eyes to new realities of warfare. World War I is still remembered as the war that shattered all of humanity's illusions and romanticism about warfare, and the *Lusitania* was just one of the episodes in that process. The world was shocked to find that war had come to a point where even civilian ocean liners could be targeted like any military vessel, with no regard to the hundreds or thousands of passengers on board. The outrage was global, with notes of protest coming even from Germany's allies.

Far from the supposedly gentlemanly gallantry of combat in the 19th century, war was no longer something that was resolved between two armies on a battlefield somewhere outside of normal, everyday life. Indeed, war was now an unstoppable destructive force that was seeping through everything, invading all areas of civilian life, never to be ignored or romanticized again. For many observers, the last notions of anything honorable or romantic in war sunk with the 1,195 souls who went down with the *Lusitania.*

Beyond shock and moral outrage, the sinking caused enormous geopolitical reverberations. The sinking of this British ocean liner was particularly relevant to the ongoing debate on America's controversial neutrality under President Woodrow Wilson in World War I. The country was looking to avoid getting involved in Europe's latest episode of mass slaughter, with the majority of public opinion agreeing that the U.S. should stay out.

The voices in favor of intervention grew over time, however, leading to the emergence of the Preparedness Movement. This was the main American campaign supporting the country's involvement in the Great War, with notable proponents being Leonard Wood and former president Theodore Roosevelt. Initially, the movement focused on increasing America's combat readiness, but it also began to function as a lobby group to get Washington to join the war effort on the side of the Entente Allies.

When 123 Americans perished with the *Lusitania,* the ensuing outrage made many Americans see Germany in a new light. Most historians agree that it isn't fair to assess the sinking as the main reason why the U.S. joined the war, but the incident undoubtedly played a major role in mobilizing public opinion against Germany and the Central Powers. Even so, it would take another two years for the U.S. to officially enter the conflict in 1917. This wasn't for lack of trying, though, as proponents of war used the *Lusitania* disaster extensively in their propaganda efforts. However, the unquestionable atrocity wasn't as clear-cut as it was portrayed by some.

At the time of her sinking, the *Lusitania* wasn't officially commandeered by the navy. This became a major point of contention in the controversy following the ship's destruction. The Germans argued that their actions were entirely legal according to the laws and customs of war. For one, they designated and announced those specific waters as a war zone, giving a clear warning to civilian shipping. They also emphasized that the ship's transportation of ammunition made it a legitimate target for their U-boats.

Legally speaking, the *Lusitania* was allowed to transport small arms ammunition, especially since it was non-explosive, in bulk. Ocean liners could carry such cargo without being registered as military vessels, and RMS *Lusitania's* cargo was declared on the manifest as per regulations. However, such fine lines do get blurred in wartime, and Germany maintained its arguments even though they apologized for the incident. The responsibility for this horrific maritime disaster remains contested to this day.

The debate has produced a wide array of interpretations and a few theories that are on the wilder side. Some believe that it was simply a misunderstanding and nothing but one of many tragedies of that terrible war. Others saw and still see the sinking as a malicious act on Germany's part. There are also those few with a more conspiratorial perspective on the incident, arguing that it might have been a carefully calculated, deliberate decision to send the *Lusitania* to its demise so as to help steer America's public opinion toward war.

The Perplexing Tunguska Incident

The Tunguska event refers to a spontaneous explosion of epic proportions that took place in the remote parts of Siberia on June 30, 1908. The yield of the explosion is estimated to have been between three and five megatons, which makes it equivalent to three to five million tons of TNT. Such a yield would make the explosion equal to a rather powerful nuclear warhead. In comparison, the two atomic weapons dropped on Japan in 1945 produced a comparatively meager 15 and 21 kilotons.

The true power of the explosion is difficult to ascertain nowadays because the instruments available to researchers in 1908 were very limited, leaving no definitive measurements in records. The power of the explosion was thus estimated in modern times based on the damage that occurred, with the most extreme estimates going up to 30 megatons.

Spontaneous Explosion in the Middle of Nowhere

Geographically speaking, the Tunguska event took place in Asia, but since Siberia was and still is part of Russia, the explosion has entered the annals of European history. It has been pondered by scientists and other curious minds throughout Europe and beyond. The many questions surrounding the event persist to this day, not just in scientific circles but also in popular culture.

The explosion completely leveled an area of 830 sq. mi. or 2,150 km², flattening around 80 million trees.

The explosion occurred at 7:17 in the morning, not far from the Podkamennaya Tunguska River in the Yeniseysk Governorate, called the Krasnoyarsk Krai in today's Russia. Across vast Siberian expanses that the human mind can hardly comprehend in their true scale, the deep Siberian wilderness is one of the most sparsely populated areas on the planet. It was only thanks to the remoteness of the location that the explosion resulted in only three deaths, as per the most accurate estimates based on equally sparse eyewitness reports. The forests of the taiga in eastern Siberia weren't as lucky as the people, as the explosion completely leveled an area of 830 sq. mi. or 2,150 km², flattening around 80 million trees.

Despite the explosion's unbelievable power, no crater was found, making it very difficult for researchers in 1908 to determine whether the explosion was caused by a meteor, a geophysical event, or something else entirely. Explorers who first arrived on the scene could see little more than miles upon miles of flattened trees, which must have been an apocalyptic sight. To see such carnage and no clear signs of what could have caused it would have certainly bewildered even the shrewdest scientific minds today, let alone in 1908.

The Tunguska event cannot be classified as a typical blunder since manmade causes could easily be ruled out. On the other hand, humanity's consistent failure to explain, beyond any doubt, what could have caused this spontaneous, seemingly natural disaster is definitely in its own category of blunder. For decades after the incident, researchers had very little to go on, but studies have produced over 1,000 scientific papers, primarily in Russian but also in other languages. Eyewitness accounts and descriptions of what happened have been well recorded and preserved to this day.

The few reports that were available shared quite a few common themes as to what could be seen in the area and the sky above during the event. An intense beam of light was commonly reported, described as having a shade of blue and being almost as bright as the sun. The light seemed to move across the sky, leaving behind a trail. As the light approached the horizon, witnesses described a blinding flash and a massive eruption of fire that seemed to split the sky in two. The entire horizon turned red as the pillar of fire lunged upward. The vertical column of fire then also split in two and gradually faded, leaving behind a black shadow in its place, likely smoke.

Demonstrating the enormity of the impact was the fact that it took around ten minutes for the sound of the explosion to reach some of the onlookers. Shockwaves followed closely behind the sound, knocking closer witnesses to the ground and smashing windows on houses hundreds of miles away. The seismic reverberations of the explosion, now believed to have been an air burst, were detected all over Eurasia. Airflow disturbances brought on by the shockwaves occurred as far away as present-day Jakarta and Washington, DC. More bizarre yet was the persistent glow in the night sky that could be observed for days in Europe and Asia. According to some reports at the time, people in Sweden and Scotland could take photographs in the dead of night without using any flashes, an impossible feat for cameras in 1908.

Theories and Speculation

Nowadays, it's theorized that the lingering light after the explosion was the result of light passing and refracting through particles of ice at high altitudes. The particles themselves are believed to have resulted from the explosion. This theory is a relatively recent one, based on similar phenomena observed during the entry of Space Shuttles into the atmosphere.

The fairly solid idea that the explosion was an air burst of an object after entering Earth's atmosphere is primarily based on the fact that no impact crater was ever found. For an object with a size large enough to produce such devastation, the crater would have been significant. The leading theories on what could have caused this mid-air explosion mostly have to do with different types of space debris entering the atmosphere and violently burning up before striking the surface.

The lack of fragments at the site has been one of the biggest problems in determining what kind of object it was. This is why a long-standing theory identified a comet, usually made of ice and space dust, as the culprit. Other theories suggested an asteroid, which is a harder object made of rock and metal, or a meteor, both of which usually burn up as they thrust through the atmosphere. Only in 2013 were scientists able to identify potentially extraterrestrial micro-samples of the disintegrated object, although work is ongoing. Various estimates have been put forth as to the potential size of this object, generally placing it at around 160 to 200 feet wide, which is around 50 to 60 meters. For all its destructive power, such an asteroid would have been minuscule in comparison to the Chicxulub asteroid, a monstrosity from outer space that wiped out the dinosaurs and left behind a 120-mile crater.

Although the asteroid hypothesis is generally accepted nowadays, the lack of clear, simple answers has given rise to legends, wild theories, and endless speculation by curious folks around the world. One local legend among the Evenki natives speaks of the supernatural origins of the explosion. An alleged witness by the name of Akulina believed that the explosion was the work of Agda, the local god of thunder. Among the rest of the Evenki tribe, the site around ground zero became a sacred place following the explosion. Some accounts even told of conflicts between the natives and the Soviet scientists who showed up to conduct research after the incident.

Aliens are another popular culprit in various theories, especially in modern popular culture. Russian writer Alexander Kazantsev proposed the hypothesis that the explosion was a nuclear detonation based on his comparisons with the devastation he had witnessed in Hiroshima, which he personally visited. Since humanity in 1908 was still quite far from developing nuclear weapons or harnessing nuclear energy, Kazancev theorized that a nuclear-powered alien spaceship exploded over Siberia. Wild theories involving secret human technologies, such as Nikola Tesla's theoretic "death ray," are also plentiful. Adding fuel to this particular theory is the fact that Tesla was indeed experimenting with such ideas around the time of the Tunguska event, attempting to wirelessly transfer energy over long distances to be used as a potential defensive weapon.

Far-fetched theories and the mystery aside, the Tunguska event is one of the best lessons nature has recently given mankind about just how vulnerable this planet and its inhabitants are to objects that run astray in space. Had the Tunguska object detonated over a major city, the death toll could have been in the millions. Even more frightening is the relatively small size of the supposed object compared to some of the other asteroids and meteors that have struck Earth over the eons. A similar reminder came on February 15, 2013, when a small air burst event occurred over the Chelyabinsk Oblast in southern Russia. The meteoroid was no more than 66 feet in diameter, and its explosion yielded around 500 kilotons. Close to 1,500 people were injured, and more than 7,000 buildings were damaged or destroyed in this well-documented incident.

Chapter 9: Pompeii's Ashes and the Flames of Hindenburg

Fiery catastrophes have been particularly well remembered across the countless blunders and disasters throughout history. Volcanic eruptions, for instance, have a special place in popular culture and fiction as well as written history. This type of natural disaster inspires fear and awe in humans on a primordial level, and with good reason. Such eruptions can reconfigure the terrain, make regions uninhabitable, and wreak untold havoc upon populated areas.

This hasn't stopped people from building their settlements in proximity to volcanoes, though. It's a conversation that has kept popping up time and time again for thousands of years, with the destruction of Pompeii in 79 AD being a widely cited example. While natural disasters can make previously prosperous areas deserted and unfit for life, manmade catastrophes can produce similar effects. A single accident can sometimes alter the way technology develops, shutting down entire industries. The *Hindenburg* airship disaster illustrates how one fateful day in air travel irretrievably damaged an entire industry. The *Hindenburg's* demise also demonstrated the power of video in shaping public opinion.

Pompeii and the Eruption of Mount Vesuvius

People don't generally establish their settlements next to active volcanoes. Most of the time, the volcano is inactive and appears like any other mountain. Volcanoes that lie dormant can be inactive for a very long time, with generations of people living around them having no idea of the danger that lurks beneath the rocks. Modern technology allows humanity to predict volcanic activity with much more accuracy, but thousands of years ago, people had little more than earthquakes to warn them in advance. Such was the story of Pompeii, an ancient Roman town in present-day Campania, Italy. Remains of this once prosperous settlement, and others in its proximity, have been preserved very well over the millennia, telling incredible stories to archeologists.

The Jewel of Roman Campania

Early settlers during the Bronze Age didn't pick the area around Mt. Vesuvius out of a hat.
https://commons.wikimedia.org/wiki/File:Napoli_Mount_Vesuvius_1858_engraving.jpg

Early settlers during the Bronze Age didn't pick the area around Mt. Vesuvius out of a hat. The climate was very agreeable, and the volcanic soil provided fertile ground for agricultural endeavors. As far as the settlers were concerned, this was a piece of prime real estate at the mouth of the Sarno River, with an imposing yet docile mountain in the background. However, interpretations of ancient Greek myths about the area might have given the Romans some insight into the region's tumultuous past.

The legends spoke of Hercules and his epic struggle with local giants against a backdrop of fire and inferno. Whether the Greeks were talking about a previous eruption of Vesuvius cannot be known to a certainty, and loose interpretations of ancient myths and legends would have hardly dissuaded the people from taking advantage of such favorable conditions to build a settlement. Still, the Herculean epic was a well-known story in the area, with one of Pompeii's neighboring towns being named Herculaneum, inspired by the Greek hero.

A permanent town began to take shape with the early Greek colonies in Campania during the 8th century BC, with other ancient peoples such as the Etruscans also making their mark. The Greeks eventually subdued such contenders in the 5th century BC while continuing to develop the town. However, the settlement was a frequent target of raids by the local Samnite people, who gradually pressured the town into submission, along with the rest of the region. The area eventually fell into disarray and infighting, which provided a window of opportunity for the Romans to start trickling in and increasing their influence.

After a rebellious period in which the Samnite-dominated town sought more independence from Rome, the city was placed under military control by Sulla in 80 BC. Thousands of Roman legionaries settled in the town, and major construction projects soon followed, turning the town into a bustling center of political and economic activity. The suburbs in the surrounding countryside also developed, with numerous villas where Roman nobility would stay on vacations. The population in Pompeii proper was probably up to 12,000, with just as many people living in the suburbs around the city. Luxurious vacation homes dotted the coast of Campania, carefully constructed to give the elite vacationers views of the sea.

Pompeii was much more than a vacation spot, however. The town was a crucial regional port serving as an export hub for goods from nearby settlements. Agricultural produce, fine products like olive oil and wine, and materials like wool, animals, and much else left the port in Pompeii and were exported throughout the vast empire. Likewise, imports played a major part in the economic activity at this essential port. Archeologists and other researchers have been able to ascertain much more about the everyday lives of people living in Pompeii. The abundance and variety of food, for instance, were particularly impressive for the world at that time.

Pompeii enjoyed infrastructural luxuries and amenities like paved roads, various shops, taverns, schools, theaters, fountains, parks, public exercise areas, temples, an amphitheater with a capacity for 5,000 people, and much more. The remains of various dwellings show that the population was divided into classes, with affordable housing for the poor strikingly different from the domiciles of the wealthy. The city also housed a significant slave population, as was the Roman custom.

The villas of Pompeii enjoyed every conceivable luxury and comfort that worldly life could offer two millennia ago.

The villas of Pompeii enjoyed every conceivable luxury and comfort that worldly life could offer two millennia ago. Short of electricity and the Internet, these lavish homes had every amenity and were designed, constructed, and decorated with incredible skill and a keenness for detail. The slaves, who might have constituted as much as a third of Pompeii's population, were nowhere near as lucky. Their housing was cramped, rudimentary, and resembled little more than a prison.

Earth's Wrath

Pompeii continued prospering until February 5, 62 AD, when previously dormant Vesuvius began to rumble. The foreboding tremors signaled that the mountain was poised to awaken from its long slumber, but the ensuing earthquake did more than warn the people. The entire immediate region around Mt. Vesuvius experienced quite a lot of devastation, with some damage occurring as far as Naples. Pompeii itself was devastated, with most structures in the city, including the defensive walls, either sustaining damage or collapsing. The earthquake and accompanying fires led to significant casualties, perhaps thousands.

Ominously, livestock in the area began dying off due to poisoning by the release of underground gases, demonstrating that this was more than just a powerful earthquake.

The terrible scourges that the earth would release upon the towns around Vesuvius would come later, however. The final eruption would occur some 17 years later, giving Pompeii just enough time to reconstruct and restore life, although a portion of the population left in the wake of the earthquake. During that time, the volcano continued hinting to the local population that it wasn't going back to sleep, but no major earthquakes or eruptions happened. The determined Romans who stayed and tried to restore the town's former glory largely ignored the occasional tremor, but the signs of impending doom would intensify in the summer of 79.

That fateful summer, the river Sarno carried dead fish, with natural springs and manmade wells evaporated and vineyards wilted. With modern seismological equipment, it probably would have been easy to predict that a major catastrophe was about to occur, but the Romans of Pompeii went about their business even when the weak but frequent tremors intensified. The inevitable transpired at some point in late summer or autumn.

The eruption process began with an explosion as the pressurized magma beneath Vesuvius' crater penetrated the surface. Initially, the onlookers in surrounding towns were simply witnesses to a giant plume of smoke emerging from the mountain, probably perplexed but still unharmed. However, the final eruption began a few hours later with another much more massive explosion. The top of the mountain was simply blown off as if from an underground nuclear bomb, and an enormous mushroom cloud ascended in its place. According to some estimates, the explosion's yield was equal to about 100,000 atomic bombings of Hiroshima.

As the awe-inspiring cloud loomed over the entire region at a height of around 27 miles, ashes began to rain down from the sky. In mere minutes, Pompeii was plastered with a thick layer of ashes that only continued to grow. The panicked residents began fleeing just to avoid being buried in the black blizzard that threatened to bury the entire city. This first onslaught alone accumulated a layer of ash whose depth was measured in meters. Unfortunately, this was just the first wave, and although the ashes buried the town, at least they were made up of tiny, lightweight particles.

The second major explosion occurred hours later, producing an even bigger discharge of ashes and debris that flew to a much higher altitude. The discharge was no longer just in the form of fine dust but rocks, some of them very heavy. People tried to seek shelter wherever they could, but the tremendous weight of accumulated ashes and debris soon began collapsing building after building. Before midnight, the massive cloud of volcanic discharge that had formed above Vesuvius could no longer support its own weight.

As it collapsed upon Pompeii and surrounding towns, the cloud released multiple waves of scorching, poisonous ash and air. The people of Pompeii, who were still alive and failed to evacuate, were being suffocated and incinerated at the same time as the volcano extinguished the last remnants of life in the town. Vesuvius continued to spew wave after wave of ashes well after the city's total destruction. By the time Vesuvius finished its apocalyptic crescendo, Pompeii was simply erased from the map and buried with thousands of its inhabitants. The continuous disregard for the many warning signs across almost two decades had finally presented its results, but the fact that Pompeii was buried so deep and so fast is one of the reasons why it was preserved so well. As nature took its toll on humanity on that fateful day, it also presented a long-term gift that would become one of the jewels of modern archeology.

The Hindenburg Disaster

Much like the Titanic, the Hindenburg was one of the marvels of its day.

Much like the *Titanic,* the *Hindenburg* was one of the marvels of its day. Air travel in the interwar period was still a novelty in many ways, but most people saw commercial zeppelins as the present and future of travel. For all intents and purposes, cross-Atlantic trips aboard zeppelins, also known as dirigibles or simply airships, resembled a voyage on an ocean liner, except in the air. One of the key advantages of airships was that they were a much faster mode of transportation. LZ 129 *Hindenburg* could make it across the ocean in half the time that the fastest ocean liners would require. The main drawback was the much smaller passenger capacity, but given the airship's catastrophic fate, this shortcoming proved to be a blessing in disguise.

A Leviathan Suspended in the Air

By the time the *Hindenburg* met her untimely demise in 1937, commercial air travel via dirigibles had been going on for around 30 years, with thousands of successful flights. Similar to how ocean liners developed around the time of the *Titanic,* newer airships placed more emphasis on various luxuries and passenger comfort. Already securing the title of the fastest way across the Atlantic, the *Hindenburg* could focus on making the trip as comfortable and opulent as possible for Germany's DZR airline clients. The designers and builders at the German Zeppelin Company envisioned each trip as being not that different from a stay in a luxury hotel. Passengers had their own comfortable cabins, which is impossible in today's most popular mode of air transport. The *Hindenburg* even had a dining area that was essentially a restaurant, with a spacious lounge and a piano to boot. For pre-war Nazi Germany, this elegant sky resort was much more than a transport aircraft. It was a symbol of Germany's impressive engineering and prestige, carrying that message not just to the United States but across North and South America.

The *Hindenburg* was the lead ship of its namesake class. She was a rigid airship, which meant that her floating body or envelope was supported by an interior skeleton, a frame that helped retain its shape. This type of airship construction is in contrast to that of usually smaller, simpler airships whose envelopes retain their shape, thanks to the pressure of the buoyant gas that fills the aerostat. LZ 129 *Hindenburg* was an enormous floating colossus. At a length of just over 803 feet (245 m), she was the largest machine that mankind had ever put into the air and the largest airship in history by its envelope's volume.

It had one fatal flaw, however. The airship was filled with and kept afloat by 7 million cubic feet (200,000 cubic meters) of hydrogen, a buoyant yet highly flammable gas. At the time of the *Hindenburg's* construction, the two main options for lifting gases in airships were hydrogen and helium. Helium was a much safer choice, as it wasn't flammable, which was a safety advantage that airship builders were well aware of. Unfortunately, helium is a rare and very expensive gas. It was so prized, in fact, that the United States passed the Helium Control Act of 1927, prohibiting its export. As helium was generally procured from only a few select oil fields in the U.S., Germany could no longer access it.

Hydrogen was a much cheaper option available to every industrialized country, and it had the added benefit of being lighter, giving the gas more lift. Even those American airships that did use helium were subject to strict regulations that necessitated great care and conservation in the use of this gas. As a result, the infinitely cheaper and lighter hydrogen seemed an obvious choice for those airship builders who were prepared to take the safety risk.

The Zeppelin Company still tried to acquire helium, even beginning the *Hindenburg's* construction with the safer gas in mind. Their hope was to acquire an American helium license at some point during construction, but the export ban remained firmly in place. Initial work thus had to be scrapped, forcing the builders to start over and build the airship for hydrogen. The two main measures that the builders took to make the airship safer were to coat the body of the blimp with a thick layer of non-flammable materials and to separate the aerostat into gas compartments.

A Historic Disaster Caught on Camera

Although the lounge areas on the *Hindenburg* included a smoking room despite the enormous amount of highly flammable gas overhead, it wasn't a stray cigarette that caused the disaster. In fact, the exact cause that triggered Hindenburg's spectacular incineration remains in contention to this day. Besides, those aboard the ship were still subject to a number of smoking rules, and the risks associated with smoking had been addressed in the airship's design.

The *Hindenburg's* fateful flight began on May 3, 1937. The enormous blimp arrived in Boston on May 6, after which she proceeded to New York City. In the afternoon hours, the airship arrived at NAES

Lakehurst, a naval air station in New Jersey, which was its final destination. The airship's captain, Max Pruss, was troubled by the weather conditions he had found there, which might have been avoided had his airship not been delayed by almost an entire day due to strong winds over Newfoundland. The unfavorable weather in New Jersey complicated a potential landing. The captain and his crew decided to spend a few hours floating along the coast of New Jersey while waiting for information on any improvements in the weather.

The letup in bad weather was but a passing respite, so the captain was advised to land the *Hindenburg* as soon as possible. What ensued was a complicated process of contending with fickle winds while trying to keep the airship's tail straight despite its inexplicable heaviness. Trying to level the vessel as it descended, the crew strategically expelled portions of the gas and water from the airship's body, but the tail kept drooping almost through the entire process. The winds picked up, and the *Hindenburg* was forced to make drastic maneuvers as it descended to the mooring area. One of the bracing wires on the airship's body had likely snapped due to the stress inflicted on it by such sharp turns, causing a breach that began an uncontrollable gas leak in one of the compartments. The *Hindenburg* still managed to approach its mooring mast and release the ropes, but the leaking hydrogen was a disaster waiting to happen.

It's uncertain as to what caused the spark that ignited the hydrogen, but the prevailing theory is that it was merely either a static discharge from the airship or an atmospheric electric spark – or a combination of both. Countless other theories were proposed during the investigation, including sabotage, but an unfortunate combination of spontaneous factors in an already dangerous situation is the most likely answer. Whatever the cause of the spark was, it took seconds for the airship to start falling after catching fire.

The tail began to collapse in on itself, and the fire rapidly spread across the compartments, contrary to the hopes of the designers, leading to a massive explosion. The entire affair was caught on video and extensively photographed, creating widespread shock and filling the media space in the following period. A total of 35 people died as the *Hindenburg* was engulfed in a massive fire and crumbled to the ground, but it was the photographic and video material that truly made the disaster stick. Despite the generally excellent safety record of airship travel before that point, people simply couldn't get over the horrific images of such a colossal flying machine burning to a crisp. Airship travel is available to enthusiasts to this day, but the *Hindenburg* disaster greatly contributed to its decline in the mainstream. Airplanes soon took over as the main mode of air transportation in spite of all the comforts and luxuries that a smooth airship voyage entails.

Chapter 10: Berlin's Barrier and Chernobyl's Catastrophe

One doesn't need to go back centuries in European history to examine major human blunders that have left an irreversible mark on the world. In just the last few decades, Europe has witnessed major events, some more catastrophic than others, but all of which have altered the course of history not just on the continent but throughout the world. Eventful as it ever was, European history continues to produce monumental shifts to this very day.

During the closing years of the Cold War, shockwaves reverberated throughout Europe on at least two well-known occasions. The first was the infamous Chernobyl disaster, which created a massive ecological disaster that could have potentially been much worse without human intervention. The second was a political turning point that came as the Berlin Wall went, ushering in a string of changes that have directly shaped life in today's Europe.

The Cold War's Microcosm in Berlin

The Berlin Wall, as a historical phenomenon, needs no introduction.
Ad Meskens, CC BY-SA 4.0 <https://creativecommons.org/licenses/by-sa/4.0>, via Wikimedia Commons: https://commons.wikimedia.org/wiki/File:Berlin_Wall_1979_02.jpg

The Berlin Wall, as a historical phenomenon, needs no introduction. It was built in Berlin during the Cold War and served as both a physical and symbolic line of separation between two very different, conflicting worlds. Common knowledge and popular perceptions usually end with the wall's purpose and its eventual fall in 1989. However, as is always the case with major historical events, there's a lot more nuance to this ideological and military wall and the ordeals of Berliners during the obstacle's existence.

A Barrier Between Two Worlds

Our lives have lost their spirit.

A petulant feeling of resignation hangs over all of us.

These were some of the descriptions of life that one resident of East Berlin, Regine Hildebrandt, wrote in her diary in the early 1960s as the construction began. Indeed, the Berlin Wall elicited many such emotions on both sides of it during its existence. It stood as a constant, daily reminder that even something as basic as movement was restricted and subject to ideological resentment between two powerful blocs.

The residents of West Berlin were essentially boxed in with a wall around the perimeter, but the citizens of West Germany who lived in the enclave could still travel freely to the rest of the FRG or any other Western or non-aligned country. This created a peculiar situation in which the East Germans often felt trapped despite the fact that East Germany physically enveloped West Berlin. The barrier, along with an intricate system of fortifications, minefields, and armed guards, lasted for almost 30 years.

This ominous manifestation of the Cold War's ideological schism in Europe was a consequence of the events following World War II. After Nazi Germany capitulated, the country was occupied by the Western Allies and the Soviets and partitioned into four zones of control. An eastern portion of Germany's current territory fell to the Soviets, while the rest was split among the U.S., UK, and France. Control over the defeated country was consolidated by the two emerging blocs in 1949, leading to the establishment of two German states. The eastern, smaller portion became the German Democratic Republic (GDR), while the rest went to the Federal Republic of Germany (FRG), which came to be known as West Germany.

While Berlin itself was captured by the Soviets and their eastern allies at the end of the war, it was agreed that this important city in the east would also be split into four zones. Just like the country, this mishmash of Allied security zones was reorganized into one eastern and one western portion a couple of years after the war. It didn't take long after the war for Europe to enter a new turbulent phase, and the Cold War was in full swing within a couple of years. The first major showdown came in 1948 when the Soviets blockaded West Berlin by cutting off all transit across East Germany. The crisis was sparked by Soviet concerns about the introduction of the new German currency by the Allies in West Berlin. After almost a year of deadlock, in which the Allies had to airdrop supplies for the citizens of West Berlin, the blockade was lifted.

While the crisis was eventually resolved, the blockade was a sign of things to come. The U.S. and USSR-led blocs could not see eye to eye even on basic economic issues such as currency, and thus, the unsustainability of the situation became apparent to everyone. Throughout the Cold War, the divided Berlin and the interstate border between East and West Germany became a major flashpoint. For decades, the entire continent and much of the world lived in constant fear that NATO and the Warsaw Pact would eventually come to blows in this divided city, leading the world into nuclear Armageddon.

Even though the Berlin Wall was built in haste, it wasn't built solely out of spite or simple hatred, although these factors played their parts. In reality, the construction was a sign of desperation more than anything else. For the communist Eastern Bloc, West Berlin was a constant thorn in its side. It interfered economically and was a glaring security and intelligence risk. It's difficult to imagine that a Soviet-controlled socialist enclave would have been welcomed with open arms somewhere in the heart of Western Europe during the Cold War. Post-revolutionary Cuba, as a communist bulwark on America's doorstep, has a long history of proving that point.

Practically speaking, East Germany had a host of other reasons to try and construct a barrier toward the West. In the aftermath of World War II, it was a devastated country crippled by economic woes and unrest. It had no way of competing with much larger West Germany and all the assistance it was receiving from the West. At a time when East Germany was supposed to rebuild itself and develop, it had to deal with a massive brain drain, losing thousands of gifted young people emigrating to the West. The same was true for less qualified workers, who were equally necessary for the reconstruction effort. This was probably the main reason why the communists decided to build a wall that, for once in history, was meant to keep people in. As per the communist officials throughout the Eastern Bloc, the wall's purpose was to protect the population from "fascist elements," preventing the will of the people through malign interference.

The Fall and Legacy

The Berlin Wall did manage to almost eliminate all emigration, so it was certainly not a blunder in that sense. Its very existence, however, symbolized a much greater historic blunder of a system that failed to retain its people. Even during the decades of the barrier, determined citizens still tried to make their way into West Berlin at great risk to their lives. The wide gap that ran along the entire wall as a security zone under the watchful eye of tower guards was eventually called the "death strip" for that very reason.

Of some 100,000 people who tried to make their way across, only around 5,000 succeeded. Most of the rest were arrested, and between 136 and 200 were shot dead while making their escape. As time passed, the would-be escapees engaged in increasingly daring and creative stunts, including tunnels, air balloons, and illicit train rides.

The emergence of the wall was sudden and shocking to many Berliners. It started with barriers and checkpoints on the early morning of August 13, 1961, and was placed at points of entry between West and East Berlin. Initial strongpoints and fences quickly gave way to concrete walls, which eventually grew to 96 miles in total length. Despite widespread international protests and quite a few tense security situations, nobody could stop the Soviet-backed GDR.

The wall's final collapse was almost as sudden as its construction, with an equally prolonged and tumultuous lead-up. A desire for democratization gripped many societies across the Eastern Bloc in the late 1980s, and Germany was a particularly intense hotspot. Massive demonstrations sprung up in the aftermath of Gorbachev's liberalization policies in the USSR, and people demanded widespread reforms. Above all, the people of Berlin wanted freedom of movement. The Berlin Wall absorbed most of that scorn as a long-standing oppressive symbol of the Iron Curtain. Among the demonstrators, some of the German activists also dared to dream of a reunified and independent Germany.

Things came to a head when Günter Schabowski, a high-ranking communist official in East Berlin, succumbed to the pressure of the protests on November 9, 1989. He intended to reach a compromise by proclaiming that the government would introduce extensive travel reforms. Protests had reached the boiling point of excitement by that point, however, and many people misconstrued Schabowski's words as an announcement that the border was now completely open. What was intended as a gradual reform immediately turned into a massive surge of people swarming the crossings all along the wall. Confusion and a communication failure paralyzed the border guards, and they simply caved to the crowd and opened the floodgates.

Crowds of East and West Berliners soon made contact for the first time in decades, and a widespread celebration ensued. Amid the outbreak of festive chaos, people simply began to tear down the wall with whatever tools they had available, and official recognition soon followed. The wall's collapse is widely regarded as the end of the Cold War, and it led to a revolutionary chain reaction across the Eastern Bloc.

To the joy of most Germans, the country was reunified the following year. Despite their previously outspoken opposition to the Berlin Wall and their anti-Soviet stance, some Western leaders viewed this historic shift with quiet anxiety. For instance, French President Mitterrand and British PM Margaret Thatcher opposed the destruction of the wall and especially the eventual reunification of Germany. In fact, Margaret Thatcher expressed her concerns to Gorbachev in September 1989, urging him to stop the wall's demolition. The wheels of history were well in motion, though, and anything short of bloodshed could not stop the process.

Chernobyl's Local Apocalypse

The nuclear incident that struck the Chernobyl region of Soviet Ukraine that fateful year is likely the most famous manmade disaster in the world today.

Since 1986, Chernobyl, also known by its Ukrainian transliteration as Chornobyl, has become a household name worldwide, albeit not for any good reason. The nuclear incident that struck the Chernobyl region of Soviet Ukraine that fateful year is likely the most famous manmade disaster in the world today. That's partly because it happened so recently, but the catastrophe and its far-reaching consequences were objectively horrendous enough to burn their mark into collective human memory. As per the International Nuclear Event Scale, the severity of the Chernobyl meltdown ranks at the highest level, seven. The recent Fukushima disaster in 2011 is the only other nuclear accident with the same dubious honor.

A Hidden Bomb in the Plant

As far as human blunders go, the Chernobyl meltdown ticked virtually every box. Nature played no hand in the disaster, and it was all mankind from start to finish. The disaster was caused by human error in operation, combined with fatal design flaws in Chernobyl's RBMK reactors. Then, after disaster struck, it was made worse through mismanagement and a string of bad decisions. It was eventually dealt with and contained, of course, but it was a bumpy ride, to say the least. Apart from being the worst peacetime nuclear disaster in history, Chernobyl is also considered by some historians as a defining moment in the late stages of the Cold War, just like the Berlin Wall.

It all began with what was supposed to be a straightforward reactor test at the Chernobyl Nuclear Power Plant, then known as the Vladimir Ilyich Lenin NPP. The experiment was to be conducted on the NPP's fourth reactor during regular maintenance on April 25, 1986, under the supervision of chief engineer Anatoly Dyatlov. The purpose of the experiment was to determine the possibility of the reactor's cooling in the event that the power plant was cut off from power.

Dyatlov, most likely motivated by his own careerism, wanted to push the reactor to its limits, leading to gross negligence and numerous violations of safety protocols. This led to a sudden surge in power, which was an immediate cause for concern among the personnel. Dyatlov's irresponsible orders eventually led to a loss of control over the reactivity in reactor four. However, he and his subordinates believed that the reactor had a failsafe that enabled it to abort the entire process if things got too unstable, and that failsafe was the infamous AZ-5 button. In normal circumstances, the button served as an emergency shutdown that would bring the reactor to a grinding halt by immediately inserting all of the control rods.

Two factors were primarily responsible for the disaster that occurred that night. First, the circumstances that arose as a result of Dyatlov's disregard for safety protocols were anything but normal. Second, the RBMK reactors used at the Chernobyl NPP had a fatal design flaw that was likely the result of cost reductions during their construction. The control rods were made of boron, which is an important element in the nuclear industry due to its ability to absorb neutrons, slowing down reactivity. Typically, operators would insert some of the many such control rods in a nuclear reactor at a certain depth when needed.

The problem with the control rods on Chernobyl's fourth reactor, like other RBMK reactors at that time, was that their tips were made of graphite, which increases reactivity. When the operators pressed the AZ-5 button to shut down the raging reactor during the surge, all 211 control rods with graphite at their tips plunged into the reactor. The button that was meant to act as a failsafe thus turned into a detonator. The moment graphite entered the core, the cooling water was vaporized into steam, which not only left the reactor without its coolant but also produced a steam explosion.

The explosion inflicted extensive structural damage on the reactor, blowing the massive lid right off the core. This allowed oxygen to rush into the core. The ensuing chemical reaction produced a second, much larger explosion that completely exposed the core. Chernobyl's reactor four immediately began spewing an endless stream of extreme radiation right into the atmosphere. None of the staff at the plant could understand what had happened or how it was possible for an RBMK reactor to simply explode like a bomb because they were oblivious to the flaws in its design.

The Cost of Lies

The liquidation effort was led by Boris Shcherbina, a senior party official, being advised by Valery Legasov and his investigative commission. Both the investigation and the efforts to deal with the disaster were hampered from the start by incompetence, state secrecy, and bureaucracy. The town and region of Chernobyl are located not far from where the present-day borders of Russia, Ukraine, and Belarus meet, so the disaster was an immediate and severe threat to all three of these Soviet republics. However, the sheer scale of the radiation being expunged into the atmosphere threatened the entire continent. It wasn't long until radioactive particles were being detected as far as Germany and Sweden, and the massive fire at the NPP was filmed by American satellites.

Even after the world discovered what was happening, the Soviet government still tried to suppress as much information as possible, making the liquidators' jobs much more difficult. Up to 24 hours after the disaster, some of the remaining reactors at the plant were still operating. The refusal to accept responsibility and the finger-pointing among the engineers and overseers at the plant greatly slowed down the initial response. The evacuation of Pripyat, a town of around 50,000 people right next to the NPP, was also delayed due to secrecy.

The town was finally evacuated on April 27 – after a whole day of residents living like nothing was going on, going about their daily business next to an active volcano of radiation. Even during the evacuation, the population was kept in the dark as to the reason behind it, being told that it was just a temporary measure. Almost 40 years later, Pripyat is one of the most famous ghost towns in the world. The Soviet authorities acknowledged the accident on April 28, but a thick shroud of mystery remained.

Luckily, the acknowledgment meant that a full-fledged national response could begin. The fact that it took until May 4 just to put out the fire speaks volumes about the intensity of the meltdown. After months of clean-up, the area around the reactor was enclosed in a sarcophagus to contain the radioactive rubble. Around 335,000 people in total were evacuated from what became the Chernobyl Exclusion Zone, which occupies around 1,000 square miles of closed-off territory with limited access.

The exact death toll has been notoriously difficult to ascertain. Fewer than 50 victims could be tied directly to the aftermath of the disaster, 28 of them killed by acute radiation sickness. The long-term death toll caused by chronic diseases, however, is probably in the thousands. The accident also wreaked havoc on the local ecosystem, leading to mutations and deformities among animals and plants.

The Zone stands to this day, and it's estimated that the area will remain uninhabitable for around 20,000 years. Not that anybody ever forgot about Chernobyl, but it made the news again in 2022 when the Zone, along with the NPP, was briefly occupied by the Russian military early in the ongoing invasion of Ukraine. During the occupation, Russian forces continued the maintenance work alongside the Ukrainians in a rare display of cooperation amid a raging war between the two post-Soviet countries.

Conclusion

As humanity marches on further into the 21st century, it's becoming increasingly clear that history hasn't stopped. In the aftermath of the Cold War, a new world seemed to emerge, at least from the Western perspective. The perception that humanity had turned some kind of monumental corner and entered into a new era where the rules and patterns of past millennia don't apply anymore became quite common. Political scientists and other thinkers such as Francis Fukuyama further articulated and popularized such notions. Fukuyama famously speculated in his 1992 book, *The End of History and the Last Man,* that the sociocultural and political development of mankind had reached an endpoint.

Over thirty years later, the world has seen such notions crumble spectacularly. Humanity has gone through major economic turmoil, embodied in the 2008 Global Economic Crisis. The world has dealt with and is still absorbing the fallout of a major ongoing pandemic caused by COVID-19, which has sent its own economic shockwaves across the planet. Last but not least, the 2022 invasion of Ukraine by the Russian Federation has triggered a worldwide geopolitical showdown that resembles a major bloc confrontation more clearly with each passing day. On top of all that, the seemingly inexorable rise of China as an economic and military colossus capable of competing with – if not surpassing the United States – is yet another challenge to the existing world order.

For better or for worse, the world is changing. The global economic system has proven itself as fragile as ever, and entire civilizations appear to be as vulnerable to major disease outbreaks as they've ever been. The security infrastructure is being questioned, eroded, and reconfigured in Europe and, consequently, elsewhere in the world. All these processes illustrate almost beyond any doubt that history has not only continued chugging along but is actually accelerating.

What this all means and where this road leads cannot be predicted beyond any doubt, but history lessons are always there to be studied and applied where possible. Some of the previously discussed stories were tales of catastrophes caused by human error, while others were nature's wrath, but all of them illustrate a few common pitfalls humanity still has to contend with. One lesson is that human endeavors, including the mightiest of empires, are transient and will eventually leave the stage.

More importantly, history's tales outline that mankind must watch out for impulsivity, poor leadership, inflexible planning, and hubris. Civilization is undoubtedly highly sophisticated nowadays, and humanity's science has never been more advanced, yet people are as fallible as ever. The most important point to take home is that the laws and patterns of history still hold true. When people built the *Titanic* and the *Hindenburg*, they thought technology had reached its peak and that nothing bad could happen. When they finalized the Treaty of Versailles, they thought World War I was so horrible that it would surely end warfare forever. The Soviets thought their nuclear industry was flawless and immune to accidents.

Complacency is the mother of all calamities, and when people take progress, comfort, safety, stability, or wealth for granted, tragedy is sure to ensue. All the wonders of the 21st century have not changed that fact, and the world is currently being reminded of that reality. Humanity's ability to escape the cycle and inherent arrogance of complacency will determine the world's ability to find its way safely into the next century. Technology, security, social stability, and world peace are not divine gifts that mankind is entitled to. They are fragile luxuries that must be treated and maintained with utmost care and humbleness.

If you enjoyed this book, a review on Amazon would be greatly appreciated because it would mean a lot to hear from you.

To leave a review:
1. Open your camera app.
2. Point your mobile device at the QR code.
3. The review page will appear in your web browser.

Thanks for your support!

Check out another book in the series

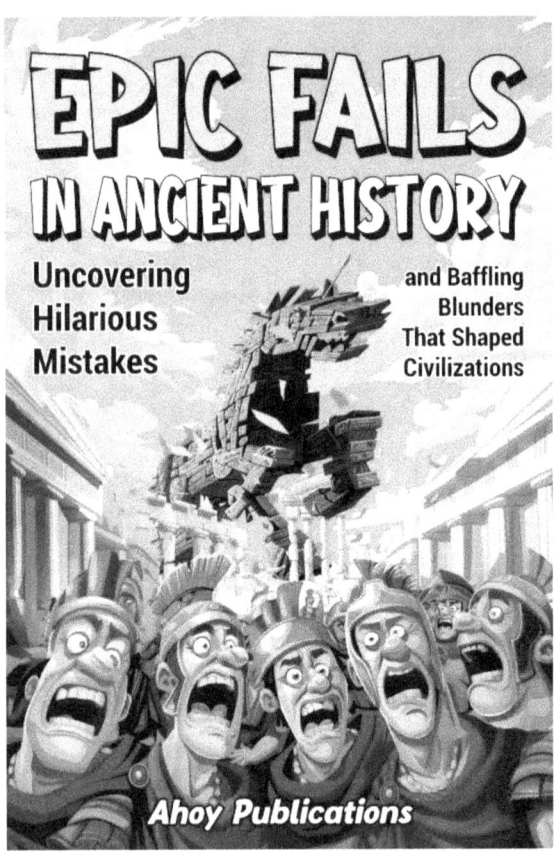

Welcome Aboard, Check Out This Limited-Time Free Bonus!

Ahoy, reader! Welcome to the Ahoy Publications family, and thanks for snagging a copy of this book! Since you've chosen to join us on this journey, we'd like to offer you something special.

Check out the link below for a FREE e-book filled with delightful facts about American History.

But that's not all - you'll also have access to our exclusive email list with even more free e-books and insider knowledge. Well, what are ye waiting for? Click the link below to join and set sail toward exciting adventures in American History.

Access your bonus here

https://ahoypublications.com/

Or, Scan the QR code!

References

Johnson, B. (2017). Great Fire of London 1666. Historic UK. https://www.historic-uk.com/HistoryUK/HistoryofEngland/The-Great-Fire-of-London/

Brain, J. (2019, July 3). The Charge of the Light Brigade. Historic UK. https://www.historic-uk.com/HistoryUK/HistoryofBritain/Charge-Of-The-Light-Brigade/

David, S. (2018, December 7). The Charge of the Light Brigade: Who Blundered in the Valley of Death? HistoryExtra; HistoryExtra. https://www.historyextra.com/period/victorian/the-charge-of-the-light-brigade-who-blundered-in-the-valley-of-death/

National Geographic, E. (2023, April 4). You Know How It Sank. How Was the Titanic Dreamed Up? National Geographic. https://www.nationalgeographic.com/premium/article/making-titanic-belfast-ship-unsinkable

Pruitt, S. (2018, August 29). Why Did the Titanic Sink? HISTORY; A&E Television Networks. https://www.history.com/news/why-did-the-titanic-sink

Ewers, J. (2008, September 25). The Secret of How the Titanic Sank. US News & World Report; U.S. News & World Report. https://www.usnews.com/news/national/articles/2008/09/25/the-secret-of-how-the-titanic-sunk

Cartwright, M. (2018, January 23). 1453: The Fall of Constantinople. World History Encyclopedia. https://www.worldhistory.org/article/1180/1453-the-fall-of-constantinople/

Cartwright, M. (2020, May 28). Spanish Armada. World History Encyclopedia. https://www.worldhistory.org/Spanish_Armada/

Cartwright, M. (2018, September 4). Children's Crusade. World History Encyclopedia. https://www.worldhistory.org/Children%27s_Crusade/

Fraga, K. (2022, March 5). In 1618, A Crowd Of Protestants Threw Three Catholics From A Window In Prague — And Sparked The Thirty Years' War (E. Hawkins, Ed.). All That's Interesting. https://allthatsinteresting.com/defenestration-of-prague

Mason, E. (2019, May 23). The 1618 Defenestration of Prague explained. HistoryExtra; HistoryExtra. https://www.historyextra.com/period/stuart/1618-defenestration-prague-facts-history-explained-what-happened-why-castle-protestant-catholic/

Ishak, N. (2021, January 12). How An "Unsinkable" Swedish Warship Found Itself At The Bottom Of The Stockholm Harbor (J. Anglis, Ed.). All That's Interesting. https://allthatsinteresting.com/vasa-ship

Wilde, R. (2019, February 6). The Treaty of Versailles: An Overview. ThoughtCo. https://www.thoughtco.com/the-treaty-of-versailles-an-overview-1221958

Bulut, M. H. (2021, October 25). Battle of Karansebes: Easiest victory in Ottoman history. Daily Sabah. https://www.dailysabah.com/arts/battle-of-karansebes-easiest-victory-in-ottoman-history/news

Dorney, J. (2016, October 18). The Great Irish Famine 1845-1851 – A Brief Overview – The Irish Story. Theirishstory.com. https://www.theirishstory.com/2016/10/18/the-great-irish-famine-1845-1851-a-brief-overview/

Mahmood, P. (2022, April 16). "Dumbest Battle In History" – Drunken Disorder And Confusion At Karánsebes. The Friday Times. https://thefridaytimes.com/16-Apr-2022/dumbest-battle-in-history-drunken-disorder-and-confusion-at-kar-nsebes

Serena, K. (2018, December 29). When The Austrian Army Fought Itself Because Its Calvary Wouldn't Share Schnapps (L. Silverman, Ed.). All That's Interesting. https://allthatsinteresting.com/battle-of-karansebes

Cartwright, M. (2023, April 5). Black Death. World History Encyclopedia; World History Publishing. https://www.worldhistory.org/Black_Death/

Mark, H. W. (2023, August 24). Napoleon's Invasion of Russia. Www.worldhistory.org. https://www.worldhistory.org/Napoleon

Homer, A. (2021, December 17). The Biggest Theories About The Tunguska Event: What Really Happened? Grunge.com. https://www.grunge.com/710556/the-biggest-theories-about-the-tunguska-event-what-really-happened/

Jay, P. (2008, June 30). The Tunguska Event. CBC. https://www.cbc.ca/news/science/the-tunguska-event-1.742329

Library of Congress. (2015). The Lusitania Disaster. The Library of Congress. https://www.loc.gov/collections/world-war-i-rotogravures/articles-and-essays/the-lusitania-disaster/

McDermott, A. (2018, April 17). How the Sinking of Lusitania Changed World War I. HISTORY. https://www.history.com/news/how-the-sinking-of-lusitania-changed-wwi

Royal Museums Greenwich. (2023, April 6). The Tunguska Event. Www.rmg.co.uk. https://www.rmg.co.uk/stories/blog/tunguska-event

Cartwright, M. (2018, March 21). Pompeii. World History Encyclopedia. https://www.worldhistory.org/pompeii/

Grossman, D. (2009). The Hindenburg Disaster. Airships.net. https://www.airships.net/hindenburg/disaster/

Stromberg, J. (2012, May 10). What Really Sparked the Hindenburg Disaster? Smithsonian; Smithsonian.com. https://www.smithsonianmag.com/science-nature/what-really-sparked-the-hindenburg-disaster-85867521/

Blakemore, E. (2019a, May 20). The Chernobyl Disaster: What Happened, and the Long-Term Impact. National Geographic. https://www.nationalgeographic.co.uk/environment/2019/05/chernobyl-disaster-what-happened-and-long-term-impact

Blakemore, E. (2019b, November 8). Why the Berlin Wall Rose—and How It Fell. National Geographic; National Geographic. https://www.nationalgeographic.com/history/article/why-berlin-wall-built-fell

www.ingramcontent.com/pod-product-compliance
Lightning Source LLC
Chambersburg PA
CBHW070726130626
46553CB00005B/2171